CHE

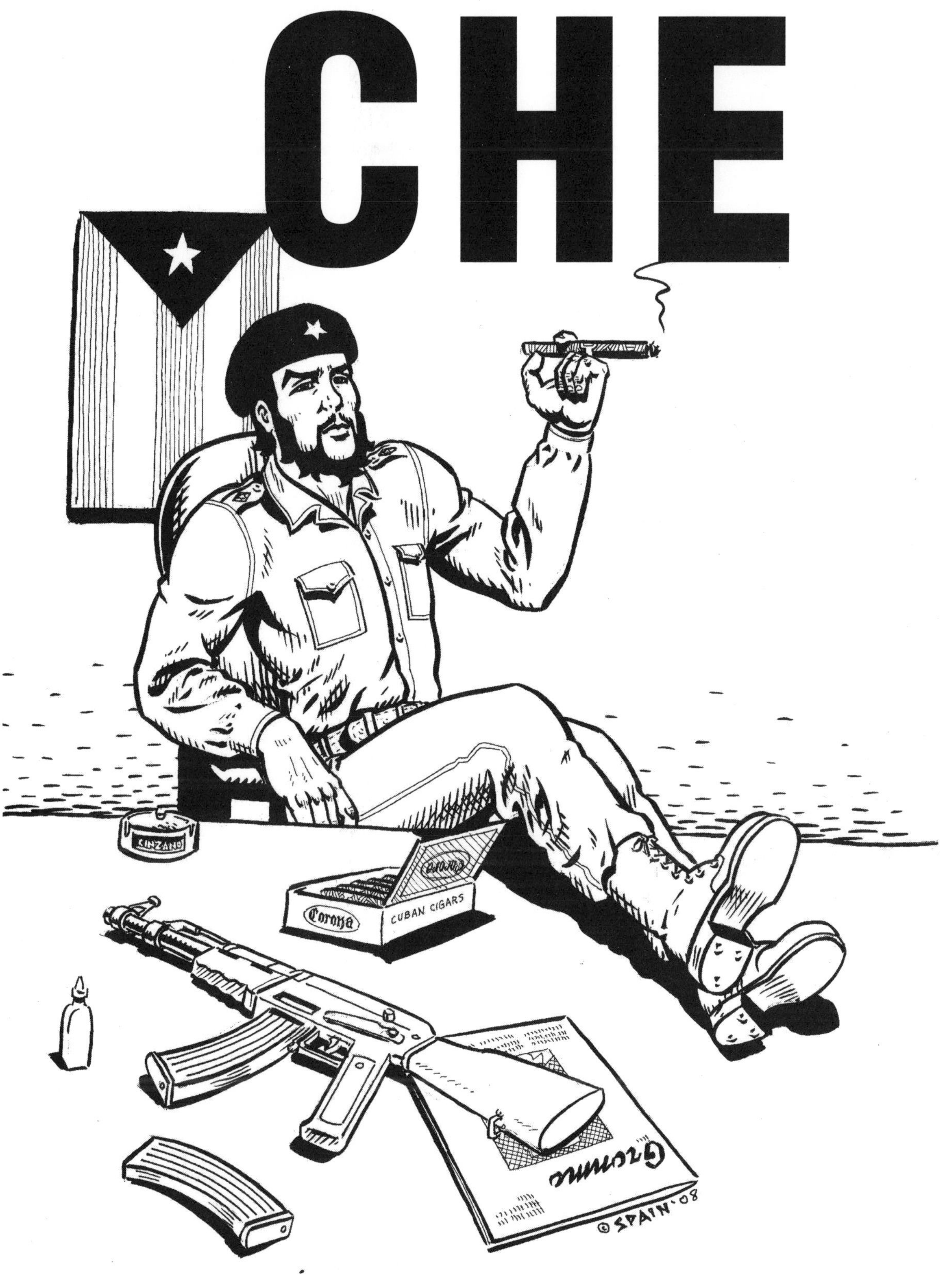
CINZANO
Corona
CUBAN CIGARS
Granma
©SPAIN·'08

CHE

A GRAPHIC BIOGRAPHY

Spain Rodriguez

edited by Paul Buhle

VERSO

London • New York

This edition published by Verso 2017
First published by Verso 2008
© Spain Rodriguez 2008, 2017

1 3 5 7 9 10 8 6 4 2

Verso
UK: 6 Meard Street, London W1F 0EG
US: 20 Jay Street, Suite 1010, Brooklyn, NY 11201

versobooks.com

Verso is the imprint of New Left Books

ISBN-13: 978-1-78663-328-6
ISBN-13: 978-1-78663-330-9 (US EBK)
ISBN-13: 978-1-78663-329-3 (UK EBK)

British Library Cataloguing in Publication Data
A catalogue record for this book is available from the British Library

Library of Congress Cataloging-in-Publication Data
A catalog record for this book is available from the Library of Congress

Typeset by Hewer Text UK Ltd, Edinburgh
Printed in the UK by CPI Clowes

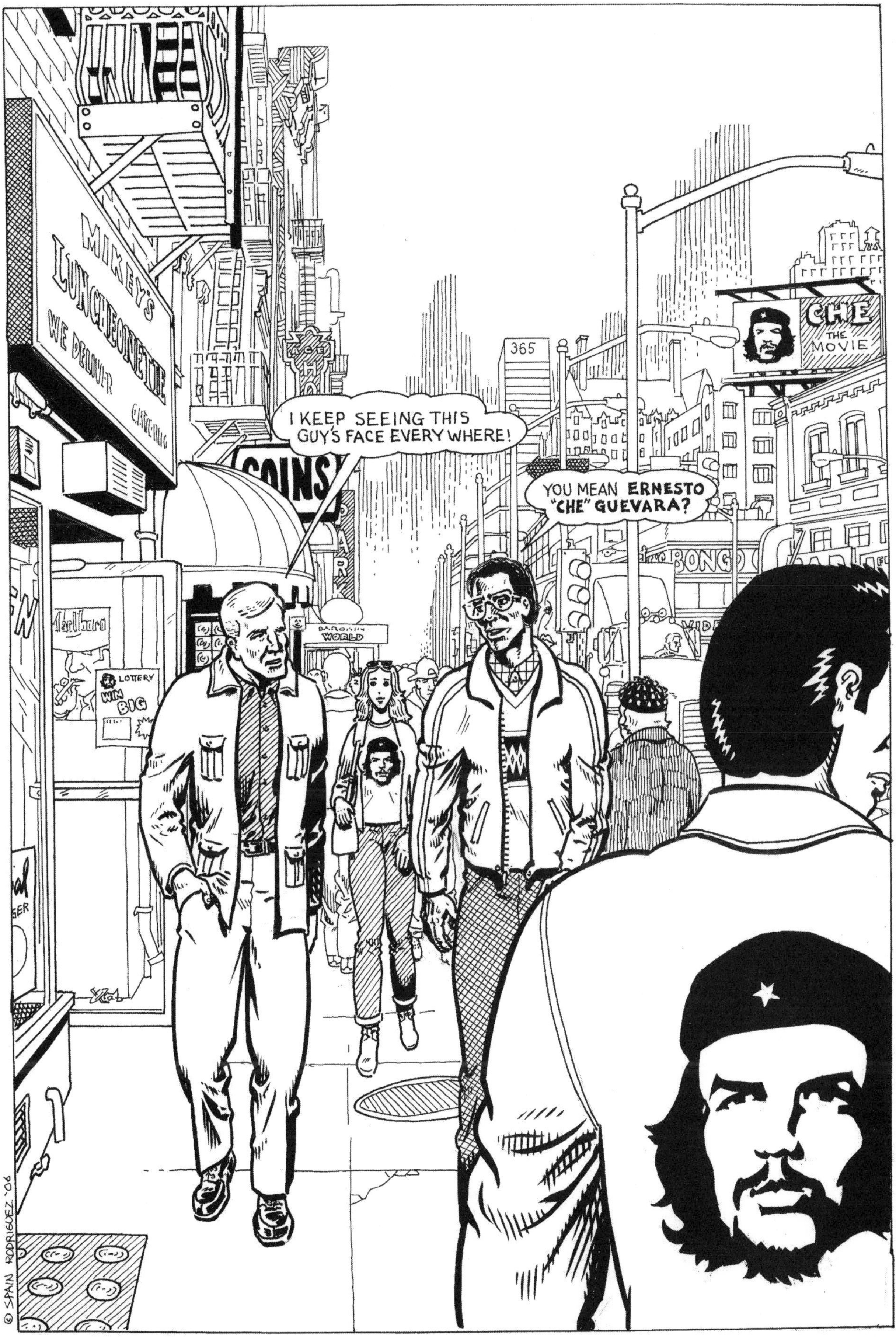
I KEEP SEEING THIS GUY'S FACE EVERY WHERE!
YOU MEAN ERNESTO "CHE" GUEVARA?
MIKEY'S LUNCHEONETTE
WE DELIVER
CATERING
COINS
365
CHE THE MOVIE
LOTTERY WIN BIG
BARGAIN WORLD
BONG
© SPAIN RODRIGUEZ '06

ERNESTO GUEVARA WAS BORN PREMATURELY ON JUNE 14, 1928 IN THE ARGENTINE CITY OF ROSARIO.

FOR CENTURIES THE HISPANIC WORLD PROVIDED REFUGE TO IRISH FLEEING PERSECUTION. GUEVARA'S MOTHER AND FATHER BOTH HAD IRISH ANCESTRY.

HE GREW UP IN A MIDDLE CLASS HOUSEHOLD, THE FIRST OF FIVE CHILDREN.

HIS PARENTS SUPPORTED THE SPANISH REPUBLIC'S LOST STRUGGLE AGAINST THE FASCIST INSURGENCY.

BUT AS THE FAMILY'S FINANCIAL FORTUNES DIMMED, THE POLITICAL ARGUMENTS GREW MORE HEATED.

CHE'S MOTHER IS RUMORED TO HAVE BRANDISHED A PISTOL DURING A FIERY POLITICAL DEBATE.

SOON, THEY MOVED TO BUENOS AIRES.

FROM AN EARLY AGE ERNESTO WAS AFFLICTED WITH CRIPPLING BOUTS OF ASTHMA.

KAHAF

THIS DIDN'T PREVENT HIM FROM PARTICIPATING IN SOMETIMES DANGEROUS GAMES WITH NEIGHBORHOOD KIDS.

THE MID-FORTIES SAW THE ASCENT TO POWER IN ARGENTINA OF FASCIST-ADMIRING GENERAL JUAN PERON.

JUAN PERON
PARTIDO ICIALISTA
PERON

AT A PERONIST DEMONSTRATION, HIS MOTHER WAS RIGHT THERE, HECKLING THE PERONISTAS.

COME ALONG SEÑORA!

SHE WAS DRAGGED OFF BY THE POLICE.

THEY PROBABLY SAVED HER LIFE.

3

PERON WAS ELECTED PRESIDENT ON FEBRUARY 24, 1946.

AT HIS SIDE WAS THE NEW FIRST LADY, FORMER ACTRESS EVA DUARTE, WHO WOULD BE KNOWN TO THE WORLD AS "EVITA".

EVITA HAD HER OWN SUPPORTERS, "THE DESCAMISADOS" OR "SHIRTLESS ONES" WHO COULD BE COUNTED ON TO BACK PERON.

UNDER PERON ALL INDUSTRIES WERE UNIONIZED. HEALTH CARE AND EDUCATION WERE FREE.

THREE MONTHS BEFORE AND THREE MONTHS AFTER GIVING BIRTH, EVERY ARGENTINE MOTHER RECEIVED PAID LEAVE.

PERON EVEN PRODUCED SOUTH AMERICA'S FIRST PROTOTYPE JET FIGHTER.

PULQUI-3

BUT THE ECONOMY SOURED AND IT WAS NEVER PUT INTO MASS PRODUCTION.

HE SOON RAN AFOUL OF THE CATHOLIC CHURCH AND ON SEPTEMBER 16, 1955 HE WAS OUSTED BY A FASCIST-MILITARY COUP.

HUELGA

ALTHOUGH HIS RHETORIC WAS SOMETIMES HARSH, THE COMMON PEOPLE BENEFITED FROM PERON'S PROGRAMS. BUT AFTERWARD THE WORKERS, UNARMED, COULDN'T DEFEND THEIR GAINS.

AS IF IN DEFIANCE OF HIS ASTHMATIC CONDITION, ERNESTO WENT OUT FOR SOCCER. HE EARNED THE NICKNAME "EL FURIBUNDO" (THE FURIOUS ONE), MAKING IT TO A SECOND DIVISION CLUB TEAM.

HE READ FROM HIS FAMILY'S EXTENSIVE LIBRARY. LATER, HE WOULD BE KNOWN AS ONE OF THE FEW MARXIST LEADERS CONVERSANT WITH FREUD.

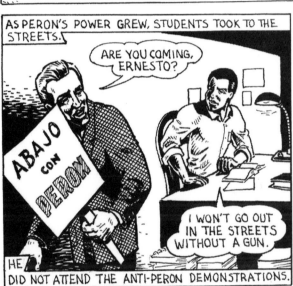

AS PERON'S POWER GREW, STUDENTS TOOK TO THE STREETS.

ARE YOU COMING, ERNESTO?

ABAJO CON PERON

I WON'T GO OUT IN THE STREETS WITHOUT A GUN.

HE DID NOT ATTEND THE ANTI-PERON DEMONSTRATIONS.

IN 1950 ERNESTO'S PARENTS SEPARATED AND HE WENT TO WORK TO CONTINUE HIS STUDIES AND SUPPORT HIS MOTHER.

ON NEW YEAR'S DAY 1950, AT THE AGE OF 22, HE SET OFF TO VISIT NEARBY NATIVE SETTLEMENTS. THEIR EXTREME POVERTY MADE A STRONG IMPRESSION ON HIM.

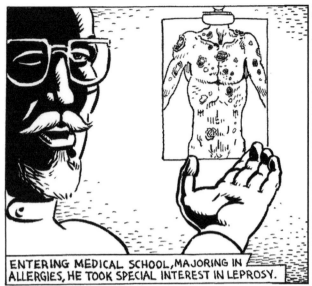

ENTERING MEDICAL SCHOOL, MAJORING IN ALLERGIES, HE TOOK SPECIAL INTEREST IN LEPROSY.

ABOUT THIS TIME HE BEGAN SEEING CHICHINA, THE DAUGHTER OF ARISTOCRATS.

WE COULD DO IT, CHICHINA. YOU AND ME, WE COULD BUILD A LIFE TOGETHER!

I... I'M SORRY, ERNESTO. THERE ARE TOO MANY DIFFERENCES. OUR FAMILIES AND...

HIS FRIEND, ALBERTO GRANADO, CONSOLED HIM.

THERE IS ONLY ONE THING TO DO AT A TIME LIKE THIS, MY FRIEND...

AND OFF THEY WENT, ACROSS THE
HIGH ANDES ON A ONE-CYLINDER
NORTON NAMED "LA PODEROSA II"
OR "THE POWERFUL ONE."

"IN NINE MONTHS OF A MAN'S LIFE HE CAN THINK A LOT OF THINGS, FROM THE LOFTIEST MEDITATIONS OF PHILOSOPHY TO THE MOST DESPERATE LONGING FOR A BOWL OF SOUP." SO BEGINS GUEVARA'S FAMOUS "MOTORCYCLE DIARIES."

ᴳ✲ᵶ!!?

SKRRRRIT

BECAUSE OF ALL THE WEIGHT ON THE BACK OF THE BIKE, IT TOOK A WHILE TO MASTER DRIVING. (NINE SPILLS IN A SINGLE DAY!)

AFTERWARDS, THEY SPENT A MISERABLE NIGHT IN A WINDSTORM THAT BLEW THEIR TENT OVER. THEY HAD TO TIE THE TENT TO A TELEPHONE POLE.

A NIGHT-WATCHMAN GAVE THEM PERMISSION TO USE A STOREHOUSE. THEY THEN WERE ABLE TO GET SOME DECENT REST.

LOOK, FELLAS. I CAN'T PAY YOU BUT TOMORROW IS THE BIG RACE AND I NEED GUYS TO HAUL FIREWOOD FOR THE BIG BARBECUE. YOU COULD HAVE ALL THE MEAT YOU CAN CARRY WITH YOU.

IT'S A DEAL.

THE NEXT MORNING, WHILE LOADING WOOD HE NOTICED THE FOREMAN HAD TAKEN A DISLIKE TO HIM.

LISTEN, CHE! DON'T PUSH DON PENDÓN TOO FAR. HE'LL GET ANGRY!

THUS ERNESTO GUEVARA WOULD GET THE NAME THAT WOULD FOLLOW HIM FOR THE REST OF HIS LIFE; "CHE" OR KID.

DESPITE A THWARTED ATTEMPT TO STEAL SOME WINE, THEY ATE WELL THAT NIGHT.

THE FOLLOWING DAY, THEY WENT OFF WELL STOCKED FOR THE NEXT LEG OF THEIR JOURNEY.

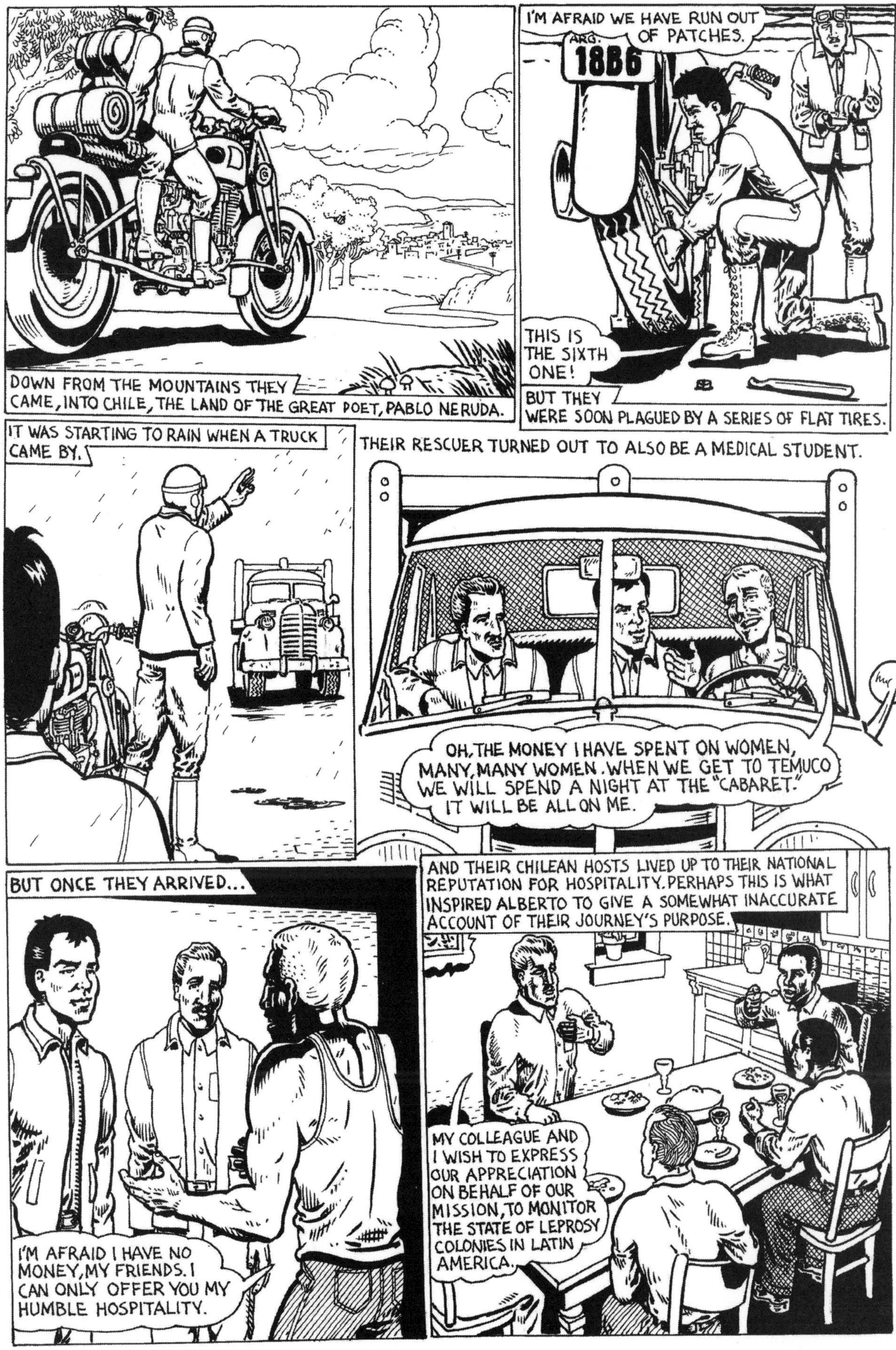
DOWN FROM THE MOUNTAINS THEY CAME, INTO CHILE, THE LAND OF THE GREAT POET, PABLO NERUDA.
I'M AFRAID WE HAVE RUN OUT OF PATCHES.
ARG.
18B6
THIS IS THE SIXTH ONE!
BUT THEY WERE SOON PLAGUED BY A SERIES OF FLAT TIRES.
IT WAS STARTING TO RAIN WHEN A TRUCK CAME BY.
THEIR RESCUER TURNED OUT TO ALSO BE A MEDICAL STUDENT.
OH, THE MONEY I HAVE SPENT ON WOMEN, MANY, MANY WOMEN. WHEN WE GET TO TEMUCO WE WILL SPEND A NIGHT AT THE "CABARET." IT WILL BE ALL ON ME.
BUT ONCE THEY ARRIVED...
I'M AFRAID I HAVE NO MONEY, MY FRIENDS. I CAN ONLY OFFER YOU MY HUMBLE HOSPITALITY.
AND THEIR CHILEAN HOSTS LIVED UP TO THEIR NATIONAL REPUTATION FOR HOSPITALITY. PERHAPS THIS IS WHAT INSPIRED ALBERTO TO GIVE A SOMEWHAT INACCURATE ACCOUNT OF THEIR JOURNEY'S PURPOSE.
MY COLLEAGUE AND I WISH TO EXPRESS OUR APPRECIATION ON BEHALF OF OUR MISSION, TO MONITOR THE STATE OF LEPROSY COLONIES IN LATIN AMERICA.

WHEN ERNESTO AND ALBERTO WENT TO FETCH THEIR TIRE THEY FOUND OUT JUST WHY THEY HAD SO MANY FLATS.

YOU HAD PIECES OF METAL EMBEDDED IN THE RIM. I TOOK THEM OUT.

FRENOS
LLANTES
CUMULADO

BUENOS DIAS, SEÑORES.

!

UНM BUENOS DIAS.

OUT ON THE STREET, PEOPLE IN THE TOWN HAD SUDDENLY BECOME MUCH FRIENDLIER.

THEY SOON FOUND OUT WHY.

☐ EL AUSTRAL ⊕

TWO ARGENTINE LEPROSY EXPERTS TOUR LATIN AMERICA BY MOTORCYCLE THEY ARE HERE IN TEMUCO

HEY, ALBERTO! TAKE A LOOK AT THIS!

IT SEEMED THAT PEOPLE HAD COMPLETELY SWALLOWED ALBERTO'S BRAGGADOCIO. EVEN WOMEN WERE FRIENDLIER.

SO THEY LEFT TEMUCO AND HEADED NORTH IN GOOD SPIRITS.

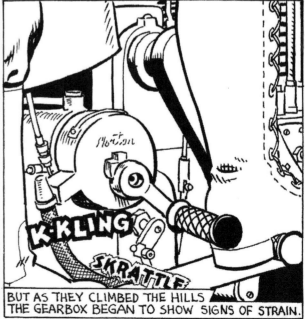

K-KLING

SKRATTLE

BUT AS THEY CLIMBED THE HILLS THE GEARBOX BEGAN TO SHOW SIGNS OF STRAIN.

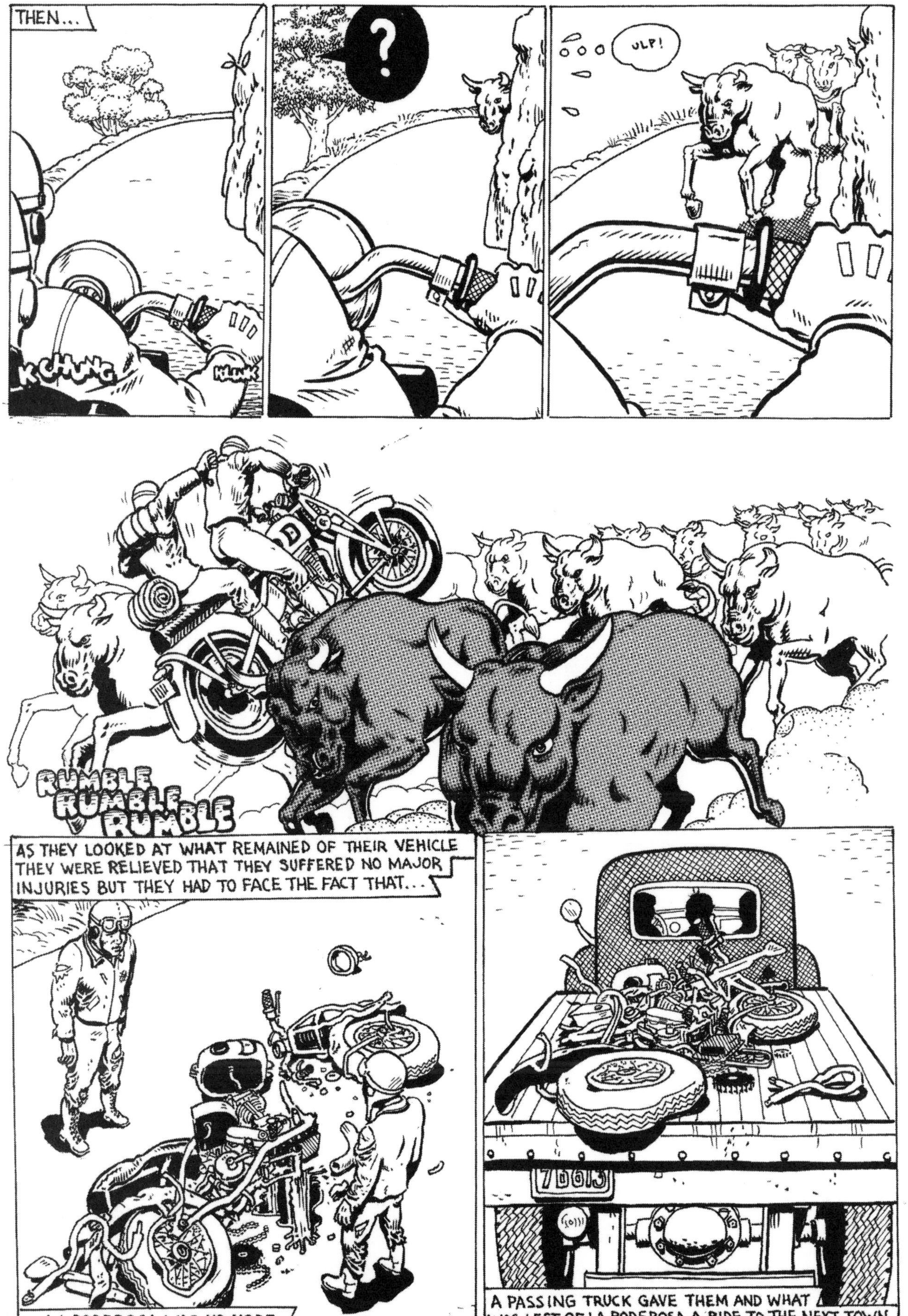
THEN...
KCHUNG
KLUNK
?
ULP!
RUMBLE RUMBLE RUMBLE
AS THEY LOOKED AT WHAT REMAINED OF THEIR VEHICLE THEY WERE RELIEVED THAT THEY SUFFERED NO MAJOR INJURIES BUT THEY HAD TO FACE THE FACT THAT...
...LA PODEROSA WAS NO MORE.
7D613
A PASSING TRUCK GAVE THEM AND WHAT WAS LEFT OF LA PODEROSA A RIDE TO THE NEXT TOWN.

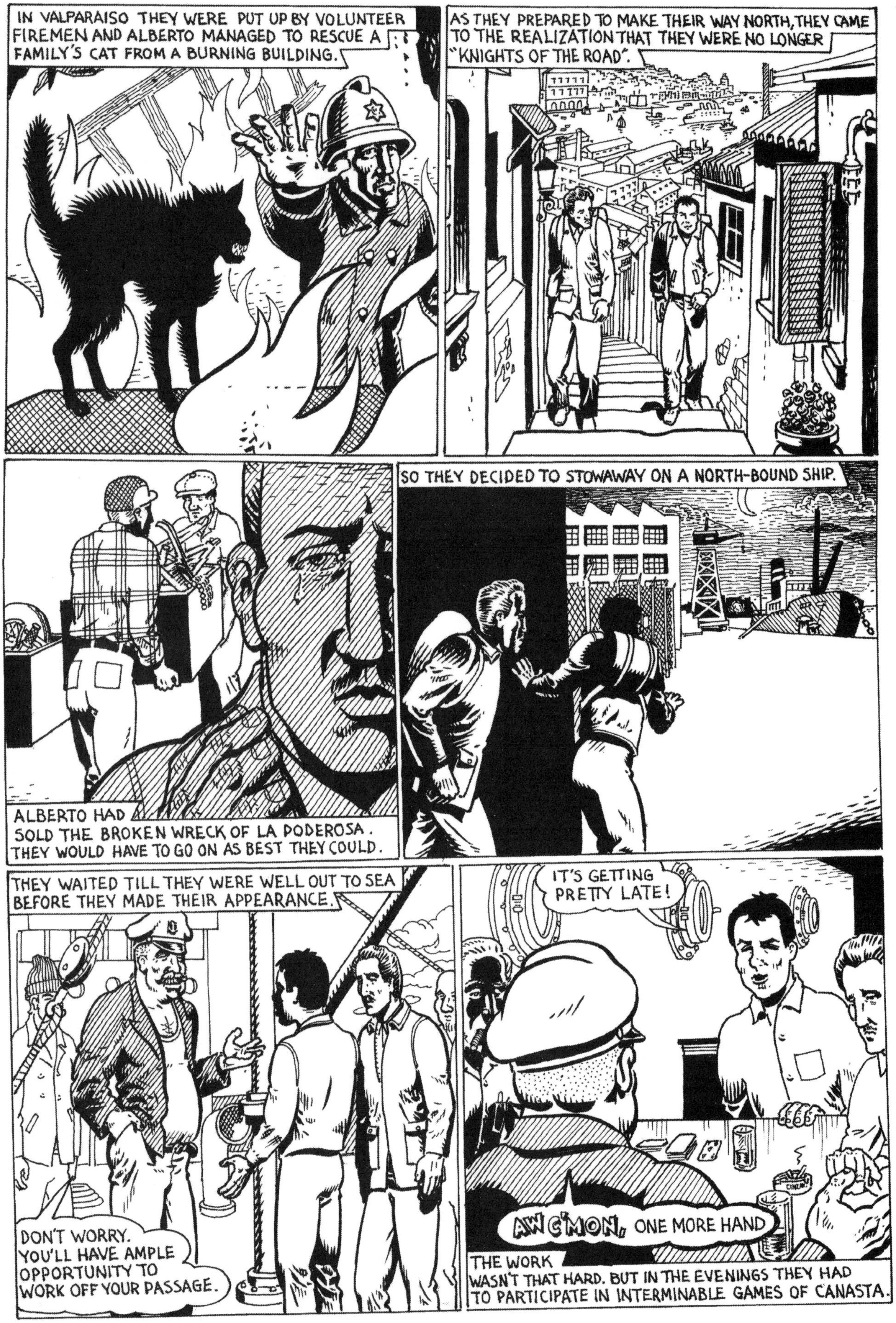
IN VALPARAISO THEY WERE PUT UP BY VOLUNTEER FIREMEN AND ALBERTO MANAGED TO RESCUE A FAMILY'S CAT FROM A BURNING BUILDING.
AS THEY PREPARED TO MAKE THEIR WAY NORTH, THEY CAME TO THE REALIZATION THAT THEY WERE NO LONGER "KNIGHTS OF THE ROAD".
ALBERTO HAD SOLD THE BROKEN WRECK OF LA PODEROSA. THEY WOULD HAVE TO GO ON AS BEST THEY COULD.
SO THEY DECIDED TO STOWAWAY ON A NORTH-BOUND SHIP.
THEY WAITED TILL THEY WERE WELL OUT TO SEA BEFORE THEY MADE THEIR APPEARANCE.
DON'T WORRY. YOU'LL HAVE AMPLE OPPORTUNITY TO WORK OFF YOUR PASSAGE.
IT'S GETTING PRETTY LATE!
AW C'MON, ONE MORE HAND
THE WORK WASN'T THAT HARD. BUT IN THE EVENINGS THEY HAD TO PARTICIPATE IN INTERMINABLE GAMES OF CANASTA.

ON THE ROAD AGAIN THEY MET A COUPLE HEADED NORTH TO THE MINES. IT WAS VERY COLD SO THEY GAVE THE COUPLE THEIR OTHER BLANKET.

HERE, TAKE THIS.

THE MAN WAS A MINER WHO HAD SPENT THREE MONTHS IN PRISON FOR BEING A COMMUNIST.

BUT PERHAPS I AM LUCKY. MANY OF MY COMPAÑEROS SIMPLY DISAPPEARED. SOME SAY THAT THEY ARE AT THE BOTTOM OF THE SEA.

THE COUPLE WENT OFF TO THE SULFUR MINES WHERE CONDITIONS WERE SO BAD THAT NO ONE ASKS ABOUT YOUR POLITICS.

EVEN IF COMMUNISTS ARE A DANGER TO "DECENT LIFE" IT SEEMS LIKE THE NATURAL LONGING FOR SOMETHING BETTER, A PROTEST AGAINST PERSISTENT HUNGER.

CREATED BY CONTROLLED DETONATIONS OF DESERT TERRAIN, THE CHUQUICAMATA COPPER MINE GRIPPED ERNESTO WITH IT'S FRIGID, GRACELESS BEAUTY.

THE MINE BOSSES WERE PREPARING FOR A THREATENED STRIKE. A MANAGER SPOKE TO THEM IN BROKEN SPANISH...

THIS NOT TOURIST TOWN, DOCTORS. BUT WE GIVE YOU A HALF-HOUR TOUR, THEN LEAVE US ALONE.

THEIR TOUR GUIDE HAD SOME COMMENTS ON THE IMPENDING STRIKE.

IMBECILIC GRINGOS, LOSING THOUSANDS OF PESOS EVERY DAY SO AS NOT TO GIVE THE WORKERS A FEW CENTAVOS.

13

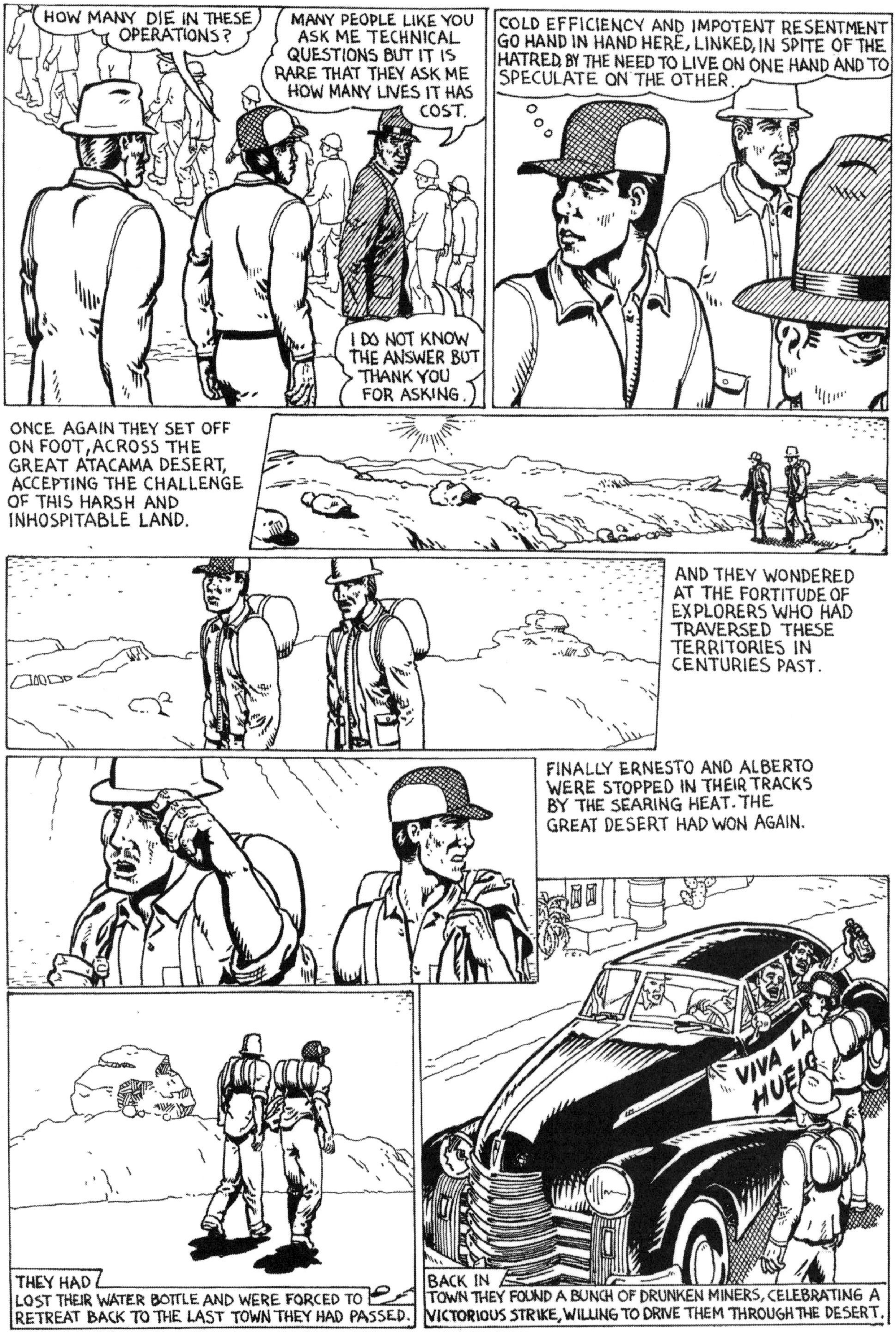

HOW MANY DIE IN THESE OPERATIONS?
MANY PEOPLE LIKE YOU ASK ME TECHNICAL QUESTIONS BUT IT IS RARE THAT THEY ASK ME HOW MANY LIVES IT HAS COST.
I DO NOT KNOW THE ANSWER BUT THANK YOU FOR ASKING.
COLD EFFICIENCY AND IMPOTENT RESENTMENT GO HAND IN HAND HERE, LINKED, IN SPITE OF THE HATRED, BY THE NEED TO LIVE ON ONE HAND AND TO SPECULATE ON THE OTHER.
ONCE AGAIN THEY SET OFF ON FOOT, ACROSS THE GREAT ATACAMA DESERT, ACCEPTING THE CHALLENGE OF THIS HARSH AND INHOSPITABLE LAND.
AND THEY WONDERED AT THE FORTITUDE OF EXPLORERS WHO HAD TRAVERSED THESE TERRITORIES IN CENTURIES PAST.
FINALLY ERNESTO AND ALBERTO WERE STOPPED IN THEIR TRACKS BY THE SEARING HEAT. THE GREAT DESERT HAD WON AGAIN.
THEY HAD LOST THEIR WATER BOTTLE AND WERE FORCED TO RETREAT BACK TO THE LAST TOWN THEY HAD PASSED.
VIVA LA HUEL
BACK IN TOWN THEY FOUND A BUNCH OF DRUNKEN MINERS, CELEBRATING A VICTORIOUS STRIKE, WILLING TO DRIVE THEM THROUGH THE DESERT.

AFTER CROSSING INTO PERU THEY SPENT A FREEZING NIGHT ON THE ROAD. IN THE MORNING THEY WERE GIVEN A FRIENDLY RECEPTION BY SOME LOCAL PEOPLE.

OH YOU'RE FROM ARGENTINA, WHERE THE POOR HAVE AS MUCH AS THE RICH AND THE INDIAN IS TREATED BETTER THAN IN THIS COUNTRY

THE NEXT DAY FOUND THEM ASCENDING INTO THE HIGH MOUNTAINS. AS THE TRUCK CLIMBED, THE WIND GREW STRONGER AND COLDER.

THEY WOULD FREQUENTLY SEE A MOUND OF STONES TOPPED BY A CROSS ON THE SIDE OF THE ROAD.

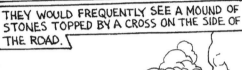

ERNESTO ASKED THE OTHER PASSENGERS ABOUT THE PRACTICE OF SPITTING OR MAKING THE SIGN OF THE CROSS AS THEY PASSED THE STONE PILES BUT NO ONE SPOKE SPANISH.

PTUI

IN ANCIENT TIMES TRAVELERS WOULD THROW A STONE AS THEY PASSED A CERTAIN SPOT TO SEND THEIR SORROWS TO PATCHAMAMA.* THEY SOON BECAME THE PILES OF STONES YOU HAVE SEEN. WHEN SPANIARDS ARRIVED, CLERICS TRIED TO ABOLISHED THE PRACTICE BUT WERE UNABLE TO DO SO. THEN THEY DECIDED TO PUT CROSSES ON THE STONE MOUNDS. NOWADAYS PEOPLE EITHER SPIT OR CROSS THEMSELVES, USUALLY THE FORMER, TO DISPENSE WITH THEIR SORROWS.

LATER IN THE DAY, THEY WERE TAKEN IN BY A TEACHER WHO HAD BEEN FIRED FOR HIS POLITICAL ACTIVITIES.

WELCOME, MY FRIENDS, FROM ARGENTINA, THE WONDERFUL LAND OF PERON.

ON THE WAY UP HERE I NOTICED PILES OF ROCKS WITH CROSSES ON TOP. PEOPLE WOULD SPIT OR CROSS THEMSELVES AS THEY PASSED BY.

* MOTHER EARTH

FAMISHED AND COLD, THEY ENTERED A BAR IN THE TOWN OF JULIACA, WHERE A DRUNKEN CIVIL GUARD SERGEANT WELCOMED THEM. THE CIVIL GUARD IN PERU HAD TREATED THEM WELL (AT ONE POST EVEN GIVING THEM EXTRA BLANKETS.)

DRINKS FOR THE GOOD DOCTORS

THANK YOU, SARGEANT.

WHAT IS THE MATTER, MY FRIEND? DO YOU NOT DRINK?

NO, NO! IT'S NOT THAT! IT'S JUST THAT IN ARGENTINA IT IS OUR CUSTOM TO DRINK ONLY AT MEALS.

TORTAS FOR THE DOCTORS AND MAKE IT SNAPPY!

THESE PEOPLE ARE ONLY KEPT IN LINE BY THE FEAR INSPIRED BY MY EXCELLENT MARKSMANSHIP. I ASSURE YOU, I AM LEGENDARY IN THESE PARTS.

THEN HE TURNED TO ALBERTO AND SAID...

WHY, I'LL GIVE YOU 20 SOLES IF I CAN'T SHOOT A CIGARETTE OUT OF YOUR MOUTH FROM ACROSS THE ROOM.

ULP

HOW ABOUT 50 SOLES

I DON'T THINK SO

NO!

100

NO WAY!

200 SOLES!

AT THIS POINT THE SERGEANT TURNED TO THE MIRROR BEHIND HIS CHAIR, TOSSED HIS HAT INTO THE AIR AND...

AH, YOU DOUBT MY ABILITIES. I SHALL SHOW YOU, THUS!

BLAM

16

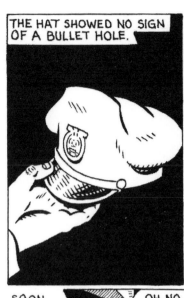

THE HAT SHOWED NO SIGN OF A BULLET HOLE.

A BULLET HOLE, HOWEVER, HAD APPEARED IN THE WALL.

NCION

MEANWHILE...
HE'S DOING IT AGAIN, JEFE. THE SERGEANT IS SHOOTING UP THE BAR.

WHA!?⑥⌀↜✱

SOON...
OH, NO, JEFE! WHAT THEY MOST LIKELY HEARD WAS THE ARGENTINIANS SETTING OFF FIRECRACKERS... YAH! THAT'S IT.

ALBERTO THOUGHT IT WAS PROBABLY BEST TO PLAY ALONG.
WHERE ARE THE FIRECRACKERS, ARGENTINIAN?

THE FIRECRACKERS UH OH, YEH! I ᵁᴴ RAN OUT.

A WOMAN FROM THE BAR PLACED HERSELF DISCREETLY IN FRONT OF THE BULLET HOLE.

THESE ARGENTINIANS. THEY THINK THEY CAN DO ANYTHING THEY WANT!

SO THEY QUICKLY LEFT. (THEY DIDN'T EVEN GET A CHANCE TO EAT THEIR TORTAS.)

SKRATCH SKRATCH

GO BACK TO WHERE YOU CAME FROM!

A FEW DAYS LATER THEY ARRIVED IN CUZCO, THE CAPITAL OF THE ANCIENT INCA EMPIRE, "THE NAVEL OF THE WORLD."

ERNESTO MUSED AT THE REMNANTS OF THE FORTRESS OF SACSAHUAMÁN

THE FIRST INCAS KNEW THIS PLACE WAS SELECTED FOR THE CHOSEN ONES WHO HAD LEFT BEHIND THEIR NOMADIC LIVES TO COME AS CONQUISTADORES TO THEIR PROMISED LAND. WITH NOSTRILS FLARING ZEALOUSLY THEY WATCHED AS THEIR FORMIDABLE EMPIRE GREW.

YET THERE IS ANOTHER CUZCO, A VIBRANT CITY WHOSE MONUMENTS BEAR WITNESS TO THE FORMIDABLE COURAGE OF THE WARRIORS WHO CONQUERED THE REGION IN THE NAME OF SPAIN AND IN THE CLEAR, SHARP FEATURES OF THE WHITE CHIEFS WHO EVEN TODAY FEEL PRIDE IN THE CONQUEST.

THE VISION OF CUZCO EMERGES MOURNFULLY FROM THE FORTRESS DESTROYED BY THE STUPIDITY OF ILLITERATE SPANISH CONQUISTADORS.

A DOCTOR THEY MADE CONTACT WITH ARRANGED FOR A CAR TO TAKE THEM TO MACHU PICCHU, THE LAST REFUGE OF THE INCAS AGAINST THE ALL-CONQUERING SPANISH FORCES. THEY ARRIVED AT DAWN.

YOU CAN EASILY APPRECIATE THE DIFFERENCE BETWEEN VARIOUS SOCIAL CLASSES, EACH ONE OCCUPYING A DISTINCT PLACE.

FROM THERE THEY WENT TO THE RE-OPENING CEREMONY OF THE CATHEDRAL OF MARIA ANGOLA. THE BELL TOWERS HAD BEEN DESTROYED BY AN EARTHQUAKE AND THE REPAIR WAS PAID FOR BY THE GOVERNMENT OF SPANISH DICTATOR FRANCISCO FRANCO.

SUDDENLY.

STOP!

TWO YEARS OF WORK AND YOU PLAY THIS?

THE CLERIC WAS OUTRAGED BECAUSE THE BAND HADN'T PLAYED THE ANTHEM OF FRANCO'S SPAIN. THEY HAD PLAYED THE ANTHEM OF THE SPANISH REPUBLIC, WHICH WAS OVERTHROWN BY FRANCO'S FASCIST REGIME, INSTEAD.

THE COUNTRY WAS MUCH GREENER NOW. THEY FINALLY CAUGHT A RIDE AFTER STANDING IN THE RAIN.

WHY NOT LET ONE OF THE WOMEN OR OLD PEOPLE SIT IN THE CAB. WE'RE OK IN THE BACK.

¡PASALE! ¡PASALE! DON'T WORRY ABOUT THEM. THEY'RE ONLY INDIANS.

KATUMM!

DIDN'T YOU SEE THAT HOLE BACK THERE? IT WAS PRETTY HARD TO MISS.

I PAID GOOD MONEY TO AVOID THE EYE TEST. MY BOSS DOESN'T CARE IF I CAN SEE AS LONG AS I DELIVER THE GOODS.

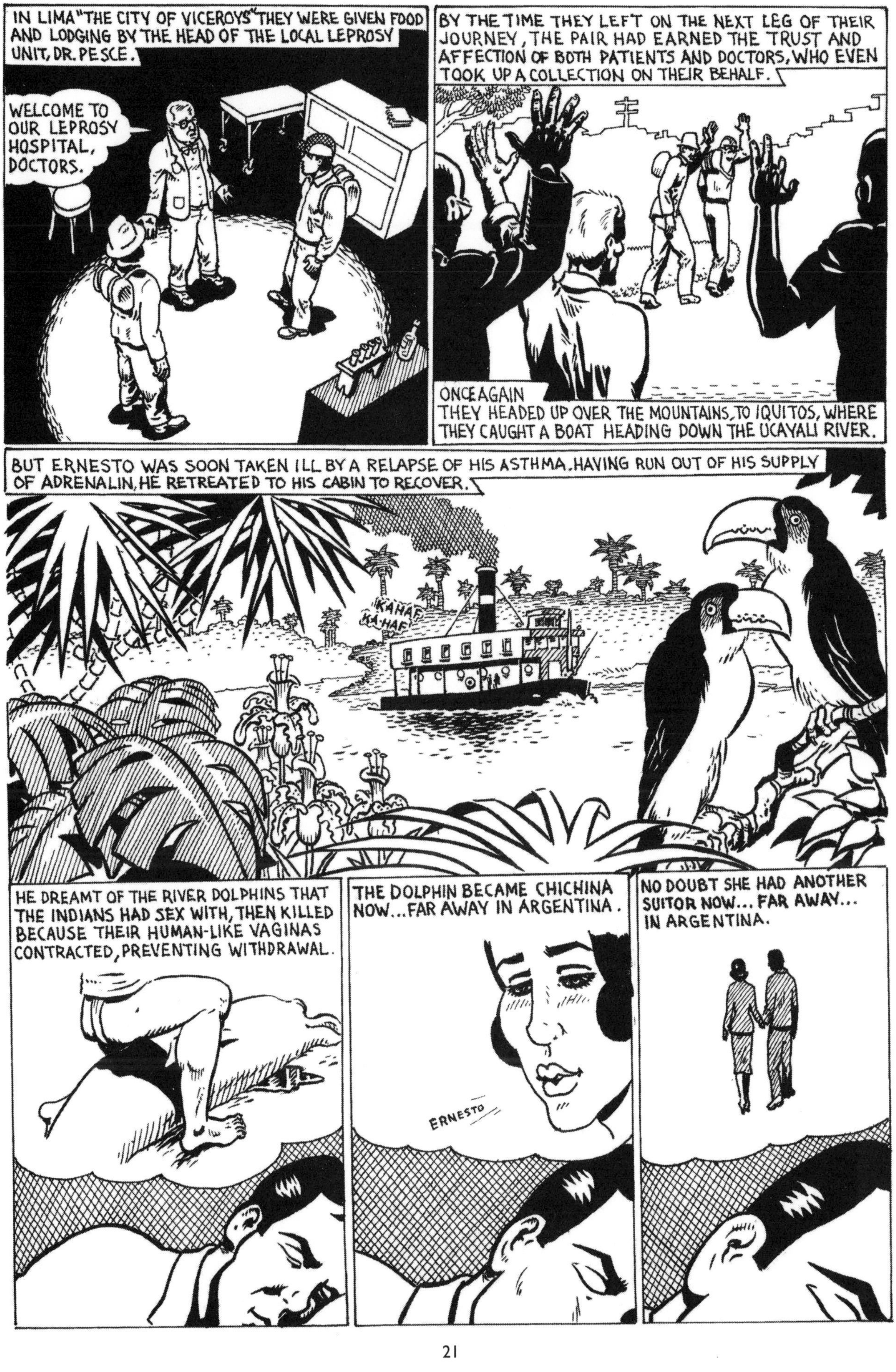

IN LIMA "THE CITY OF VICEROYS" THEY WERE GIVEN FOOD AND LODGING BY THE HEAD OF THE LOCAL LEPROSY UNIT, DR. PESCE.
WELCOME TO OUR LEPROSY HOSPITAL, DOCTORS.
BY THE TIME THEY LEFT ON THE NEXT LEG OF THEIR JOURNEY, THE PAIR HAD EARNED THE TRUST AND AFFECTION OF BOTH PATIENTS AND DOCTORS, WHO EVEN TOOK UP A COLLECTION ON THEIR BEHALF.
ONCE AGAIN THEY HEADED UP OVER THE MOUNTAINS, TO IQUITOS, WHERE THEY CAUGHT A BOAT HEADING DOWN THE UCAYALI RIVER.
BUT ERNESTO WAS SOON TAKEN ILL BY A RELAPSE OF HIS ASTHMA. HAVING RUN OUT OF HIS SUPPLY OF ADRENALIN, HE RETREATED TO HIS CABIN TO RECOVER.
KAHAF
KA-HAF
HE DREAMT OF THE RIVER DOLPHINS THAT THE INDIANS HAD SEX WITH, THEN KILLED BECAUSE THEIR HUMAN-LIKE VAGINAS CONTRACTED, PREVENTING WITHDRAWAL.
THE DOLPHIN BECAME CHICHINA NOW... FAR AWAY IN ARGENTINA.
ERNESTO
NO DOUBT SHE HAD ANOTHER SUITOR NOW... FAR AWAY... IN ARGENTINA.

THEY ARRIVED AT THE SAN PABLO LEPER COLONY ON SUNDAY AND THE WHOLE STAFF TURNED OUT TO GREET THEM.

THE COLONY WAS EFFICIENTLY ADMINISTERED BY A NUN CALLED SISTER ALBERTO.

SISTER ALBERTO HAD OTHER CONCERNS.

BEEN TO CHURCH LATELY?

I HAVEN'T SEEN YOU AT MASS, ERNESTO.

IN ITS EARLY STAGES LEPROSY IS QUITE VIRULENT. ERNESTO AND ALBERTO HAD STUDIED THIS DISEASE EXTENSIVELY. THEY UNDERSTOOD THAT WHEN THE SORES WERE HEALED THE DISEASE WASN'T CONTAGIOUS. ALTHOUGH THE PATIENTS WERE USED TO BEING AVOIDED AND SHUNNED, HUMAN CONTACT WAS GREATLY APPRECIATED.

AS ERNESTO AND ALBERTO CONTINUED TO "MISS MASS" THEY STARTED TO NOTICE THAT THEIR FOOD SERVINGS AT DINNER HAD BEGUN TO SHRINK.

FORTUNATELY TODAY, BECAUSE OF THE ADVANCES OF SCIENCE, THERE ARE FEW YOUNG LEPERS. BUT THE PEOPLE OF THE COLONY WERE GRATEFUL FOR EFFORTS OF THE TWO TO IMPROVE THEIR LOT. THEY THREW A PARTY ON THE EVE OF THE PAIR'S DEPARTURE AND ERNESTO GAVE A TOAST.

ALTHOUGH OUR INSIGNIFICANCE MEANS WE CAN'T BE SPOKESPEOPLE FOR SUCH A NOBLE CAUSE, WE BELIEVE AFTER THIS JOURNEY MORE FIRMLY THAN EVER, THAT THE DIVISION OF LATIN AMERICA INTO UNSTABLE AND ILLUSIONARY NATIONS IS COMPLETELY FICTIONAL. WE CONSTITUTE A SINGLE MESTIZO RACE WHICH FROM MEXICO TO THE MAGELLAN STRAIGHTS BEARS ETHNOGRAPHICAL SIMILARITIES.

ERNESTO USED HIS EXPERTISE IN SOCCER TO TRAIN THE LOCAL TEAM, TRANSFORMING THEM INTO REGIONAL CHAMPIONS.

AND SO, IN AN ATTEMPT TO RID MYSELF OF THE WEIGHT OF SMALLMINDED PROVINCIALISM, I PROPOSE A TOAST TO PERU AND TO A **UNITED LATIN AMERICA!**

ON FRIDAY THEY DEPARTED DOWN THE RIVER ON A RAFT CALLED THE "MAMBO-TANGO" BUILT BY THE INHABITANTS OF SAN PABLO.

THE CURRENT IS TOO **SWIFT!**

WE'RE NOT GOING TO MAKE IT.

AS THEY NEARED THE TOWN OF LETICIA THE RAFT HEADED FOR MID-RIVER. IT SEEMED TO HAVE A MIND OF ITS OWN, SURGING PAST THEIR DESTINATION.

EVENTUALLY THEY MADE IT TO A PLACE WHERE THEY COULD CATCH A BUMPY FLIGHT TO BOGATA, COLOMBIA, AND FROM THERE TO VENEZUELA.

THE AUTHORITIES IN VENEZUELA WERE NOT AS FRIENDLY AS IN THE OTHER COUNTRIES THEY HAD VISITED.

AT THAT TIME VENEZUELA WAS UNDER DICTATOR PEREZ JIMÉNEZ, A U.S. STATE DEPARTMENT FAVORITE.

ONCE AGAIN THEY TRAVERSED THE MOUNTAINS, THIS TIME TO CARACAS IN A BUS PRONE TO FLAT TIRES.

FRAP

ERNESTO CAME DOWN WITH ANOTHER ATTACK OF ASTHMA AND ALBERTO INJECTED HIM WITH ADRENALIN.

ON THE STREETS HE SAW THE INTERACTIONS OF AFRICAN AND PORTUGUESE NEWCOMERS WITH OBSERVATIONS THAT WOULD TODAY BE CONSIDERED RACIST.

THE BLACK IS INDOLENT AND A DREAMER; SPENDING HIS MEAGER WAGE ON FRIVOLITY AND DRINK. THE EUROPEAN HAS A TRADITION OF WORK AND SAVING, WHICH HAS PURSUED HIM AS FAR AS THIS CORNER OF AMERICA AND DRIVES HIM TO ADVANCE HIMSELF.

ON A STARRY NIGHT IN A CARACAS SLUM HE ENCOUNTERED A WORLD TRAVELER.

THE FUTURE BELONGS TO THE PEOPLE, AND GRADUALLY, OR IN ONE STRIKE, THEY WILL TAKE POWER HERE AND IN EVERY COUNTRY.

THE TERRIBLE THING IS PEOPLE NEED TO BE EDUCATED, AND THIS THEY CANNOT DO BEFORE TAKING POWER. THEY CAN ONLY LEARN AT THE COST OF THEIR OWN MISTAKES, WHICH WILL BE VERY SERIOUS AND WILL COST MANY INNOCENT LIVES, OR PERHAPS NOT, MAYBE THOSE LIVES WILL NOT HAVE BEEN INNOCENT BECAUSE THEY WILL HAVE COMMITTED THE HUGE SIN AGAINST NATURE; MEANING LACK OF ABILITY TO ADAPT. YOU AND I, FOR EXAMPLE, WILL DIE CURSING THE POWER THEY HELPED WITH GREAT SACRIFICE TO CREATE. REVOLUTION IS IMPERSONAL. MY SIN IS GREATER BECAUSE I, MORE ASTUTE, WILL DIE KNOWING THAT MY SACRIFICE STEMS ONLY FROM AN INFLEXIBILITY SYMBOLIZING OUR ROTTEN CIVILIZATION. I ALSO KNOW YOU WILL DIE WITH YOUR FIST CLENCHED AND YOUR JAW TENSED, A PERFECT MANIFESTATION OF STRUGGLE.

ERNESTO'S VIEW OF THE WORLD WAS CHANGING.

ERNESTO GUEVARA WENT BACK TO ARGENTINA TO FINISH HIS MEDICAL STUDIES. HE WOULD RETURN TO CONTINUE HIS WANDERINGS SOMETIMES WITH ALBERTO, SOMETIMES WITH OTHERS.

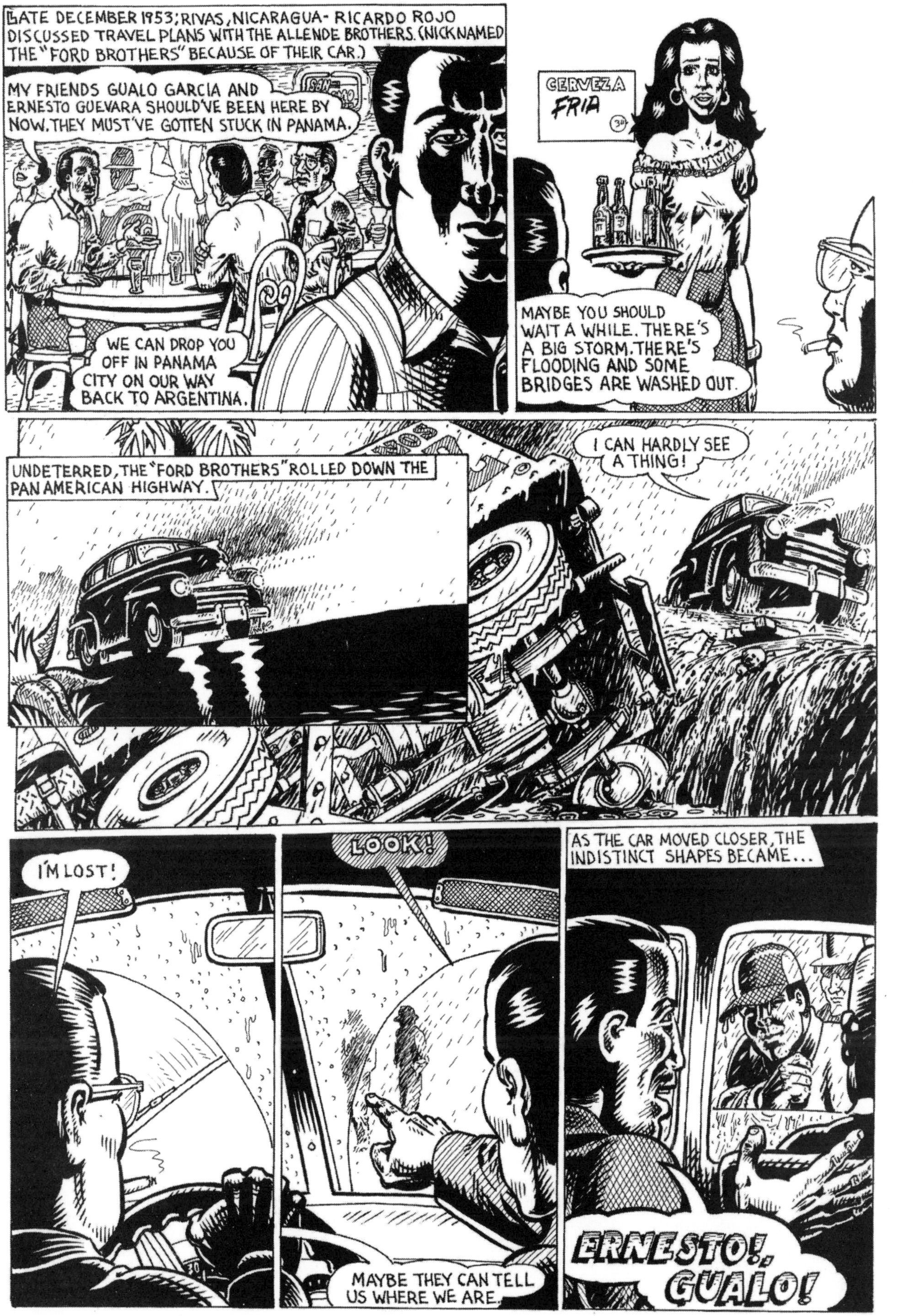

LATE DECEMBER 1953; RIVAS, NICARAGUA- RICARDO ROJO DISCUSSED TRAVEL PLANS WITH THE ALLENDE BROTHERS. (NICKNAMED THE "FORD BROTHERS" BECAUSE OF THEIR CAR.)
MY FRIENDS GUALO GARCIA AND ERNESTO GUEVARA SHOULD'VE BEEN HERE BY NOW. THEY MUST'VE GOTTEN STUCK IN PANAMA.
WE CAN DROP YOU OFF IN PANAMA CITY ON OUR WAY BACK TO ARGENTINA.
CERVEZA FRIA
MAYBE YOU SHOULD WAIT A WHILE. THERE'S A BIG STORM. THERE'S FLOODING AND SOME BRIDGES ARE WASHED OUT.
UNDETERRED, THE "FORD BROTHERS" ROLLED DOWN THE PAN AMERICAN HIGHWAY.
I CAN HARDLY SEE A THING!
I'M LOST!
LOOK!
MAYBE THEY CAN TELL US WHERE WE ARE.
AS THE CAR MOVED CLOSER, THE INDISTINCT SHAPES BECAME...
ERNESTO!, GUALO!

THERE'S NO MORE ROAD AHEAD. EVERYTHING HAS BEEN WASHED OUT, BRIDGES, EVERYTHING.

SO THE "FORD BROTHERS" DROVE EVERYONE BACK TO RIVAS.

CENTRAL AMERICA AT THAT TIME WAS IN A STATE OF POLITICAL FERMENT. ERNESTO AND HIS FRIEND SOON MADE CONTACT WITH A GROUP CALLED THE CARIBBEAN LEGION."

THE UNITED STATES HAS A FRIENDLY FACE THAT PROMISES UNDERSTANDING, AND AN IMPERIALIST FACE I WILL FIGHT.

BUT, SEÑOR BETANCOURT* THIS DICHOTOMY SETS UP FALSE CHOICES THAT CAN ONLY BENEFIT THE POWERFUL.

*RÓMULO BETANCOURT BECAME PRESIDENT OF VENEZUELA 1958-1963

IDEALISTIC YOUNG MEN FROM ALL OVER LATIN AMERICA HAD BEEN GIVEN MILITARY TRAINING. THEY HAD CARRIED OUT A SERIES OF INEFFECTIVE ATTACKS AGAINST GENERAL TRUJILLO, RULER OF THE DOMINICAN REPUBLIC REFERRED TO AS "OUR SON OF A BITCH" BY DWIGHT EISENHOWER.

AMONG THE GROUPS PRESENT WAS THE CUBAN JULY 26 MOVEMENT.

WHILE IT IS TRUE THAT OUR ATTACK ON THE MONCADA BARRACKS FAILED AND OUR LEADERS HAVE BEEN CAPTURED, THE CUBAN PEOPLE ARE BEGINNING TO RISE.

THE DICTATOR BATISTA HAS HAD TO RESORT TO MASSACRING STUDENTS, WORKERS, AND PEASANTS ALL OVER CUBA.

ERNESTO WAS SKEPTICAL.

NOW TELL ME A COWBOY STORY.

ON THEIR WAY THROUGH EL SALVADOR THEY VISITED A COLONEL VIDEZ.

A RECOMMENDATION FROM AMBASSADOR FUÑEZ IS A WORTHY RECOMMENDATION INDEED!

FROM THE WINDOW, THE COLONEL'S LOVELY DAUGHTER SHOWED THEM A VIEW OF THE ESTATE.

THE NEXT DAY, ON THE TOUR OF THE ESTATE, GUEVARA SAW THE OPERATION UP CLOSE.

IT ALL LOOKED VERY EFFICIENT.

THAT EVENING THE GUESTS ENJOYED THE COLONEL'S SUMPTUOUS HOSPITALITY.

TO OUR ESTEEMED NEW FRIENDS, WELCOME TO OUR HUMBLE HOME.

THE LOVELY DAUGHTER NOTICED ERNESTO'S DISCOMFORT.

SOMETIMES THE PEASANTS ARE DISOBEDIENT AND LACK AFFECTION FOR THEIR WORK. WE HAVE OUR INTERNAL POLICE AND THEIR DUTY IS TO RESTORE ORDER AT THE FIRST SIGN OF REBELLION FROM THOSE PEOPLE.

LATER, HER FATHER CLARIFIED.

YOU THINK I EARNED THIS COLONEL'S RANK AT A MILITARY ACADEMY? TWENTY-FIVE YEARS AGO THEY ROSE UP. IT WAS I WHO DID THE KILLING WHEN THE KILLING HAD TO BE DONE.

THEY ALL LEFT THE NEXT MORNING.

PAPA IS A GOOD MAN.

27

WHEN THEY ARRIVED IN GUATEMALA IN MID-JANUARY, 1954, THEY COULD FEEL A SENSE OF ALARM AND UNREST.

ON JANUARY 29, 1954, ELECTED PRESIDENT JACOBO ARBENZ MADE THIS ACCUSATION.

AN INVASION OF GUATEMALA IS BEING PLOTTED BY A GOVERNMENT TO THE NORTH.*

* HE DIDN'T MEAN MEXICO.

THE C.I.A.'S PRESENCE SEEMED EVERYWHERE IN THOSE DAYS.

ERNESTO OFFERED HIS SERVICES AS A DOCTOR FOR WORK IN RURAL AREAS.

YOU DON'T HAVE YOUR P.G.T.* CARD? I'M AFRAID THIS INTERVIEW IS OVER.

LOOK, FRIEND, THE DAY I DECIDE TO AFFILIATE MYSELF, I'LL DO IT FROM CONVICTION NOT OBLIGATION, UNDERSTAND?

P.G.T. GUATEMALAN WORKERS PARTY - THE COMMUNIST PARTY.

IT WAS A TIME OF FESTIVITIES IN GUATEMALA CITY.

WHY DON'T YOU JOIN US, HILDA?

NO, I DON'T FEEL LIKE IT NOW. I'LL SEE YOU AT THE PARTY.

SOMETIME LATER.

YOU MUST BE ONE OF THOSE ARGENTINIANS I'VE HEARD SO MUCH ABOUT.

YOU MUST BE HILDA GADEA. YOU SEEM TO KNOW EVERYONE.

28

ERNESTO INVITED HILDA TO A COMMEMORATION OF THE ASSASSINATION OF AUGUSTO SANDINO. A HIGH GOVERNMENT OFFICIAL WAS ALSO IN ATTENDANCE.

I SEE THAT THE MINISTER DID NOT COME HERE WITH HIS WIFE.

IF THEY TOLD ME HE WAS LEAVING HIS WIFE FOR SOMEBODY LIKE YOU, A THINKING WOMAN, THAT WOULD BE ALL RIGHT, BUT TO CHANGE ONE PRETTY FACE FOR ANOTHER MAKES NO SENSE.

SOON THEIR COMMON SENSIBILITIES CONCERNING POETRY AND POLITICS BECAME SOMETHING DEEPER.

AFTER HIS ELECTION IN 1950, PRESIDENT JACOBO ARBENZ BEGAN A PROGRAM TO MODERNIZE AND EXPAND GUATEMALA'S PORT FACILITIES.

IN JUNE OF 1952 HE INSTITUTED A LAND REFORM PROGRAM THAT CONFISCATED UNUSED FARM LAND, PAYING OWNERS THE PRICE THEY CLAIMED THEIR LAND WAS WORTH ON THEIR TAX ASSESSMENTS. THE LARGEST LAND OWNER WAS THE UNITED FRUIT COMPANY. ARBENZ CLAIMED ITS LAND WAS WORTH ONLY $3 AN ACRE. 85% OF ITS LAND WAS IDLE.

THIS ENRAGED THE UNITED FRUIT COMPANY.

JUST WHO THE **HELL** DO THEY THINK THEY ARE?

THE UNITED FRUIT COMPANY DEMANDED THAT THEY BE PAID $75 AN ACRE.

REPUBLICAN SENATOR HENRY CABOT LODGE, WHO HAD EXTENSIVE HOLDINGS IN UNITED FRUIT, WAS INFORMED.

WHA!!?... JUST WHO DO THEY THINK THEY ARE?

WORD SOON GOT OUT TO SECRETARY OF STATE JOHN FOSTER DULLES AND HIS BROTHER, ALLEN, HEAD OF THE CIA, BOTH OF WHOM HAD EXTENSIVE HOLDINGS IN UNITED FRUIT.

WE'LL SHOW THEM JUST WHO THEY'RE DEALING WITH!

SOON.

ERNESTO WAS SURPRISED TO LEARN THAT PERON HAD ORDERED ALL ARGENTINIAN CRUISE SHIPS TO STOP AT GUATEMALAN PORTS IN RESPONSE TO AN AMERICAN BOYCOTT OF THAT COUNTRY'S TOURISM.

HILDA TOOK CARE OF ERNESTO AS THE HEAT AND DAMPNESS AGGRAVATED HIS CONDITION.

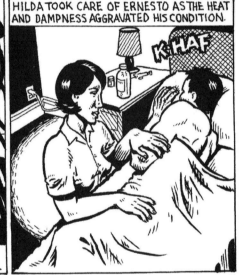

IN JUNE OF 1954 A CIA-SPONSORED COUP PUT AN END TO THE ADMINISTRATION OF GUATEMALA'S SECOND FREELY ELECTED PRESIDENT.

THIS USHERED IN A SERIES OF BLOODY DICTATORSHIPS THAT LASTED FOR OVER 40 YEARS, PUNCTUATED BY FREQUENT REVOLTS, AND MASSACRES OF THE LOCAL POPULATION.

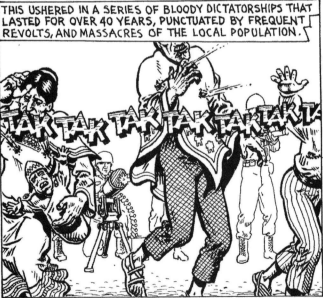

AFTER THE COUP, ANYONE SUSPECTED OF COMMUNIST SYMPATHIES WAS ARRESTED. GUEVARA AND HIS FRIENDS FLED TO THE ARGENTINIAN EMBASSY.

THEY SOON SLIPPED INTO MEXICO.

AT THIS POINT ERNESTO'S THINKING WAS UNDERGOING A PROFOUND TRANSFORMATION. ...HE WAS BECOMING "CHE."

AFTER THE FALL, THE COMMUNISTS WERE THE ONLY ONES WHO STILL KEPT THEIR FAITH AND CAMARADERIE AND ARE THE ONLY GROUP WHO CONTINUED THEIR WORK. IT'S CLEAR THAT ANY COMPROMISE WITH THE UNITED STATES IS IMPOSSIBLE.

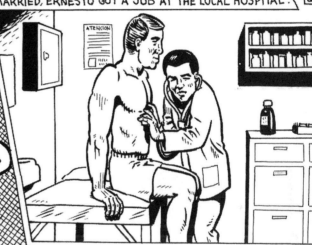

HILDA JOINED ERNESTO IN MEXICO AND, AFTER THEY WERE MARRIED, ERNESTO GOT A JOB AT THE LOCAL HOSPITAL.

HILDA GADEA WAS A WOMAN WHO HAD A BROAD UNDERSTANDING OF POLITICS. SHE HAD A PROFOUND EFFECT ON THE EVOLUTION OF GUEVARA'S IDEAS.

SHE HERSELF WAS IN EXILE BECAUSE SHE HAD BEEN A LEADER OF THE MARXIST WING OF A.P.R.A., A LEFT PERUVIAN PARTY.

ON FEBRUARY 15, 1956, ERNESTO'S DAUGHTER, HILDITA, WAS BORN.

HILDA HAD CONTACTS WITH POLITICAL EXILES FROM ALL OVER LATIN AMERICA. THROUGH HER, HE MET RAUL CASTRO AND EVENTUALLY..

I WOULD LIKE YOU TO MEET MY BROTHER. **FIDEL.**

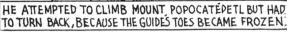
ERNESTO STILL FELT CALLED TO WILD PLACES.

HE ATTEMPTED TO CLIMB MOUNT POPOCATÉPETL BUT HAD TO TURN BACK, BECAUSE THE GUIDE'S TOES BECAME FROZEN.

HILDA SUPPORTED HIS DECISION TO JOIN FIDEL CASTRO'S JULY 26 MOVEMENT AND GO OFF FOR MILITARY TRAINING.

ERNESTO "CHE" GUEVARA TURNED OUT TO BE A CRACK SHOT.

BLAM

HIS FEELINGS DEEPENED DURING HIS STAY IN MEXICO CITY, "THE CAPITAL OF CORRUPTION."

MEXICO IS ENTIRELY GIVEN OVER TO THE YANKEES. LABOR LEADERS HAVE BEEN BOUGHT OFF AND SIGN UNFAIR CONTRACTS IN RETURN FOR SUPPRESSING STRIKES.

CUBANS HAD BEEN BATTLING THE MILLION-MAN SPANISH ARMY FOR DECADES, WHEN THE UNITED STATES DECIDED TO INTERVENE IN 1898.

SOON AFTER THEODORE ROOSEVELT CHARGED THE OUTNUMBERED DEFENDERS OF SAN JUAN HILL, THE UNITED STATES WON AN OVERSEAS EMPIRE AT THE COST OF FEW HUNDRED DEATHS INFLICTED BY SPANIARDS. *

BUT CUBANS THEMSELVES FAILED TO ACHIEVE TRUE INDEPENDENCE.

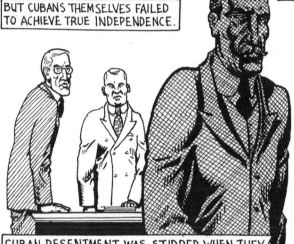

CUBAN RESENTMENT WAS STIRRED WHEN THEY WERE MADE TO SIGN THE PLATT AMENDMENT, GIVING THE U.S. THE RIGHT TO SEND ITS MILITARY INTO CUBA ANYTIME IT WISHED.

CUBA ABROGATED THE PLATT AMENDMENT IN 1934

RESENTMENT WAS EXACERBATED WHEN A DRUNKEN AMERICAN SAILOR URINATED ON A STATUE OF CUBAN POET-LIBERATOR, JOSE MARTI.

DURING THIS PERIOD AN URBAN PROFESSIONAL CLASS GREW, AIDED BY AN AMERICAN-BUILT INFRASTRUCTURE SUCH AS ROADS AND SCHOOLS.

THE COUNTRY SIDE, HOWEVER, REMAINED MIRED IN POVERTY, TIED LARGELY TO A SINGLE CROP: SUGAR.

* IN CONTRAST, THOUSANDS OF TROOPS DIED FROM TAINTED BEEF SUPPLIED BY AN AMERICAN MEAT COMPANY.

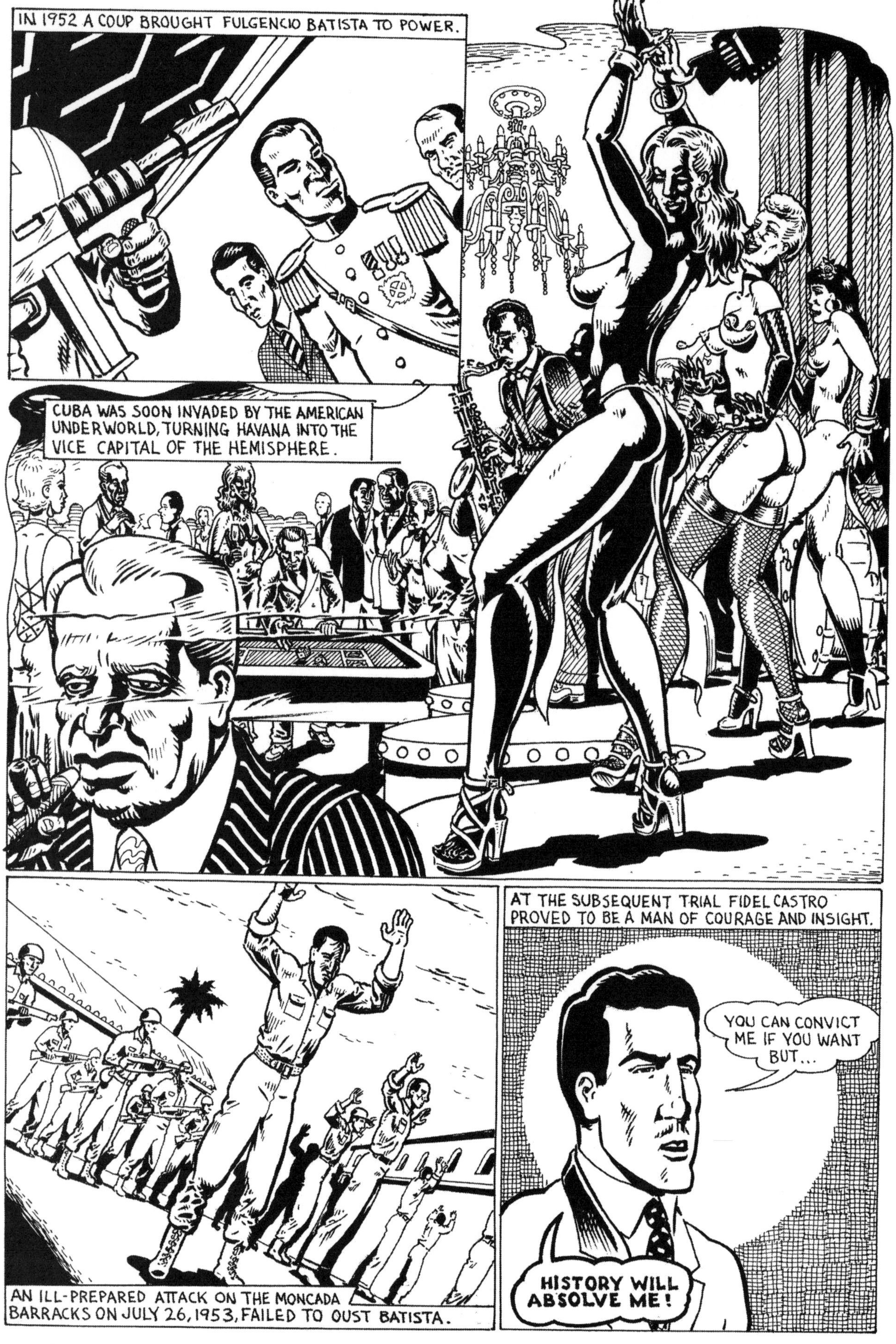
IN 1952 A COUP BROUGHT FULGENCIO BATISTA TO POWER.
CUBA WAS SOON INVADED BY THE AMERICAN UNDERWORLD, TURNING HAVANA INTO THE VICE CAPITAL OF THE HEMISPHERE.
AN ILL-PREPARED ATTACK ON THE MONCADA BARRACKS ON JULY 26, 1953, FAILED TO OUST BATISTA.
AT THE SUBSEQUENT TRIAL FIDEL CASTRO PROVED TO BE A MAN OF COURAGE AND INSIGHT.
YOU CAN CONVICT ME IF YOU WANT BUT...
HISTORY WILL ABSOLVE ME!

BATISTA ISSUED A GENERAL AMNESTY IN 1955 AND CASTRO WAS RELEASED. HE RETURNED TO MEXICO WHERE HE MET ERNESTO.

AFTER AN ALL-NIGHT CONVERSATION FIDEL WAS SUFFICIENTLY IMPRESSED TO GIVE HIM COMMAND OF A BRIGADE.

PREFIGURING HIS FINAL MISSION, GUEVARA POSED AS AN ARGENTINE BUSINESSMAN TO RENT THE RANCH WHERE THE INSURGENTS WOULD BE TRAINED.

COLONEL ALBERTO BAYO, A VETERAN OF THE SPANISH REPUBLIC'S DOOMED STRUGGLE AGAINST FASCISM, AIDED THE PREPARATIONS.

THE TRAINING PROCESS WAS INTENSE.

BESIDES MARKSMANSHIP, ERNESTO SHOWED EXCEPTIONAL ABILITY AND DISCIPLINE AS WELL.

DID YOU SEE "EL CHE ARGENTINO" OUT THERE? HE REALLY TORE UP THE FIELD.

THE NICKNAME "CHE" (SPANISH FOR "HEY YOU" OR "KID") THAT HE HAD AQUIRED EARLIER BEGAN TO STICK.

BUT THESE ACTIVITIES DID NOT GO UNNOTICED BY MEXICAN AUTHORITIES.

THEY CAN'T BE UP TO ANY GOOD.

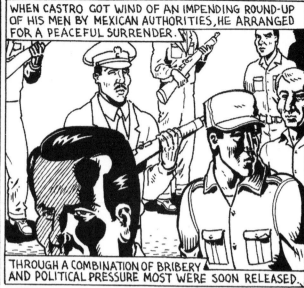

WHEN CASTRO GOT WIND OF AN IMPENDING ROUND-UP OF HIS MEN BY MEXICAN AUTHORITIES, HE ARRANGED FOR A PEACEFUL SURRENDER.

THROUGH A COMBINATION OF BRIBERY AND POLITICAL PRESSURE MOST WERE SOON RELEASED.

CHE (AS HE WAS NOW CALLED BY HIS CUBAN COMRADES) REMAINED IN JAIL BECAUSE HE HAD ENTERED THE COUNTRY ILLEGALLY.

THE REVOLUTION SHOULD NOT IN ANY WAY BE IMPEDED ON MY ACCOUNT. I UNDERSTAND THE SITUATION AND I WILL TRY TO FIGHT FROM WHAT EVER COUNTRY THEY SEND ME TO.

I WILL NOT ABANDON YOU!

AND HE DIDN'T. LATER ON, CASTRO LAID OUT WHAT HAD TO BE DONE.

TIME HAS RUN OUT. WE MUST MAKE OUR MOVE.

IN NOVEMBER 1956, 82 MEN SET SAIL FOR CUBA ON THE YACHT "GRANMA."

THE GRANMA SLIPPED SILENTLY OUT OF THE HARBOUR AT TUXPAN AND HEADED FOR THE DARK CARIBBEAN.

BUT THEN...

MAN OVERBOARD!

FIDEL ORDERED THE BOAT TO GO BACK BUT THEY COULD FIND NO TRACE OF HIM.

IT'S TOO DARK. WE'LL NEVER FIND HIM.

KEEP SEARCHING!

FINALLY THE FEEBLE CRIES OF EX-NAVY LIEUTENANT ROQUE WERE HEARD AND HE WAS PULLED BACK ON BOARD.

ALREADY BEHIND SCHEDULE AND TAKING ON WATER THE GRANMA LEFT THE GULF OF MEXICO.

BUT THEY WERE SPOTTED AS THEY ENTERED CUBAN WATERS.

AT A DESIGNATED LANDING SPOT REINFORCEMENTS AWAITED THEM...

ALONG WITH VEHICLES TO TAKE THEM INTO THE MOUNTAINS.

BUT THEY WERE FORCED TO LAND IN A MANGROVE SWAMP, 40 MILES FROM THEIR DESTINATION.

ON THEIR WAY TO THE INTERIOR, FARMERS OFFERED THE HUNGRY MEN FOOD.

SUDDENLY...

BLAM BLAM

KRAK

BLAM BLAM

POK

POK

TWANG

TAK TAK TAK TAK TAK TAK TAK

THEY HAD BEEN BETRAYED BY THEIR GUIDE.

BRAKA BRAKA B

TAKATATAT

BLAM BLAM BAM POP

El Mercurio

BATISTA FORCES CRUSH REBELS

THOSE WHO COULD, FLED, CARRYING THE WOUNDED. THE REST WERE CUT DOWN OR CAPTURED.

BACK IN MEXICO HILDA FRANTICALLY SEARCHED FOR NEWS OF ERNESTO.

BAMF

TAK TAK TAK

AS THEY BROKE UP INTO SMALL GROUPS, HEADING TO THEIR MOUNTAIN RETREAT, CHE WAS HIT IN THE NECK.

ONLY A FEW MADE IT TO THE SIERRA MAESTRA MEETING PLACE. INCLUDING CHE, FIDEL AND RAUL CASTRO, 15 HAD SURVIVED THE DEADLY WELCOME.

EXHAUSTED AND DEMORALISED, THE INSURGENTS ASSESSED THEIR SITUATION.

FIDEL ADDRESSED HIS DISPIRITED MEN.

WE HAVE SUFFERED GREAT LOSSES TO GET HERE. GOOD MEN HAVE DIED.

BUT WE HAVE SURVIVED AND SOON, WITH THE PEOPLE OF CUBA **WE SHALL TRIUMPH!**

WORD OF THE FATE OF THEIR CAPTURED COMRADES SOON GOT BACK TO THE REBELS.

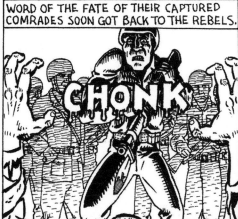

CHONK

BATISTA'S PACIFICATION CAMPAIGN IN THIS IMPOVERISHED REGION QUICKLY BECAME AN EXCUSE TO MISTREAT THE LOCAL POPULATION.

AT FIRST CASTRO AND HIS MEN WERE RELUCTANT TO MAKE CONTACT WITH THE PEASANTS FOR FEAR SOMEONE WOULD TURN THEM IN.

THEIR DIET AT THIS TIME CONSISTED MOSTLY OF BOILED YUCCA WITHOUT SALT.

BUT THEY QUICKLY FOUND A WARM RECEPTION FROM THE PEOPLE OF ORIENTE PROVINCE, TIRED OF THE ARMY'S ABUSIVE TACTICS.

WELCOME, WELCOME!

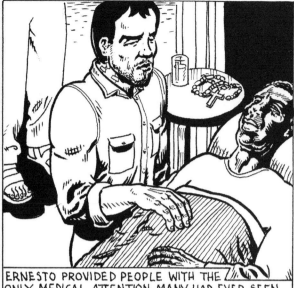

ERNESTO PROVIDED PEOPLE WITH THE ONLY MEDICAL ATTENTION MANY HAD EVER SEEN.

THREE WEEKS AFTER THEIR ARRIVAL IN THE SIERRA MAESTRA, THE REBELS LAUNCHED A SUCCESSFUL ATTACK ON A MILITARY BARRACKS IN THE COASTAL VILLAGE OF LA PLATA.

EJERCITO CUBANO

FIDEL CASTRO ENFORCED A STRICT POLICY OF GOOD TREATMENT OF CIVILIANS, INCLUDING PAYMENT FOR ANYTHING TAKEN.

SOON THEIR RANKS BEGAN TO SWELL WITH RECRUITS FROM SURROUNDING AREAS.

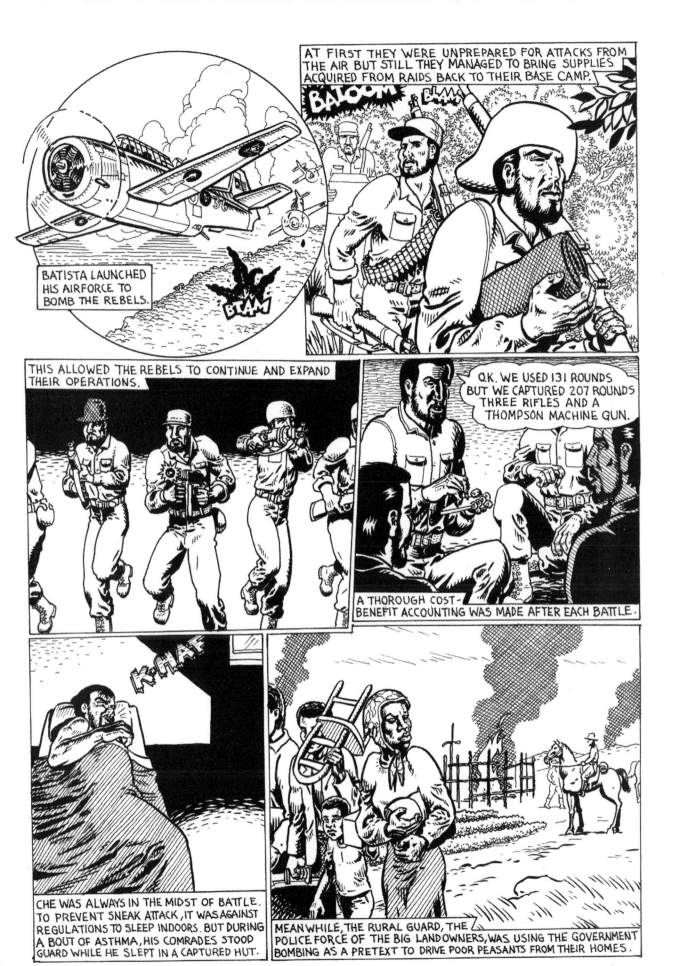

BATISTA LAUNCHED HIS AIRFORCE TO BOMB THE REBELS.

AT FIRST THEY WERE UNPREPARED FOR ATTACKS FROM THE AIR BUT STILL THEY MANAGED TO BRING SUPPLIES ACQUIRED FROM RAIDS BACK TO THEIR BASE CAMP.

BAIOOM BLAM

BTAM

THIS ALLOWED THE REBELS TO CONTINUE AND EXPAND THEIR OPERATIONS.

O.K. WE USED 131 ROUNDS BUT WE CAPTURED 207 ROUNDS THREE RIFLES AND A THOMPSON MACHINE GUN.

A THOROUGH COST-BENEFIT ACCOUNTING WAS MADE AFTER EACH BATTLE.

K-HAF

CHE WAS ALWAYS IN THE MIDST OF BATTLE. TO PREVENT SNEAK ATTACK, IT WAS AGAINST REGULATIONS TO SLEEP INDOORS. BUT DURING A BOUT OF ASTHMA, HIS COMRADES STOOD GUARD WHILE HE SLEPT IN A CAPTURED HUT.

MEANWHILE, THE RURAL GUARD, THE POLICE FORCE OF THE BIG LANDOWNERS, WAS USING THE GOVERNMENT BOMBING AS A PRETEXT TO DRIVE POOR PEASANTS FROM THEIR HOMES.

IN FEBRUARY, 1957, NEW YORK TIMES REPORTER HERBERT MATTHEWS CAME TO THE SIERRA MAESTRA TO INTERVIEW FIDEL CASTRO.

SOON THE WORLD KNEW THAT THE CUBAN REVOLUTION WAS ALIVE AND HILDA KNEW THAT ERNESTO HAD SURVIVED.

REBELS IN SIERRA MAESTRE

BUT THE LIFE OF A GUERRILLA WAS NOT FOR EVERYONE.

I WAS PROMISED ANTI-AIRCRAFT PROTECTION AND PLENTY OF FOOD.

THOSE WHO STAYED QUICKLY LEARNED THAT THE GUERRILLA FACED A LIFE OF DANGER AND PRIVATION.

EVENTUALLY THEY WERE HONED INTO AN EFFECTIVE FIGHTING FORCE BY SPANISH CIVIL WAR VETERAN COLONEL ALBERTO BAYO.

CHE WAS APPROACHED BY A PEASANT-RECRUIT NAMED JULIO ZENON WHO WANTED TO LEARN TO READ.

ONE MORNING EUTIMIO GUERRA AWOKE. HE SAID HE HAD A DREAM.

I DREAMT THAT THE PLANES ATTACKED LOMO DEL BURRO.

THE NEXT DAY AT LOMO DEL BURRO...

IT'S JUST LIKE IN EUTIMIO'S DREAM!

JULIO ZENON WAS IMPRESSED. EUTIMIO HAD MADE OTHER PREDICTIONS THAT HAD TURNED OUT.

I HAVE HEARD OF PEOPLE SUCH AS THIS. THEY CAN SEE THINGS WE CAN NOT!

VIEWS LIKE THIS WERE GIVEN MUCH CREDENCE. IT WAS CHE'S JOB TO DISPEL THESE IDEAS.

IT'S JUST NOT POSSIBLE TO TELL THE FUTURE THROUGH DREAMS. COINCIDENCES OCCUR. WE CANNOT SUCCUMB TO MAGICAL THINKING.

LATER ON, EUTIMIO ASKED TO GO ON LEAVE.

MY GRANDMOTHER IS SICK. I NEED TO GO SEE HER.

HOW LONG WILL YOU BE GONE?

ABOUT TWO WEEKS.

A FEW DAYS LATER.

KEEP OUT OF SIGHT! IT'S AN ARMY OBSERVATION PLANE!

THEY DIDN'T SUSPECT THAT FLYING IN THE PLANE ABOVE THEM WAS EUTIMIO.

...AND THAT'S WHERE YOU WILL FIND THEIR BASE CAMP!

43

AFTER A WHILE EUTIMIO'S BEHAVIOR BEGAN TO AROUSE SUSPICION.

HOW MANY MEN ARE ON WATCH TONIGHT?

JULIO ZENON WAS GUNNED DOWN BY BATISTA AIRCRAFT WHILE ON PATROL. THEY SEEMED TO KNOW RIGHT WHERE HE WOULD BE.

THEN THE GUERRILLAS TALKED TO THE LOCAL PEOPLE.

THAT'S RIGHT. EUTIMIO GUERRA WENT OVER TO THE SIDE OF THE GOVERNMENT.

...AND AFTER HE WAS CAPTURED BY COLONEL CASILLAS HE WAS OFFERED MONEY AND MILITARY RANK TO KILL FIDEL CASTRO.

WHEN THEY CAUGHT UP WITH EUTIMIO, HE FREELY CONFESSED EVERTHING.

I...I KNOW YOU'RE GOING TO SHOOT ME.

CHE WAS DESIGNATED TO CARRY OUT THE EXECUTION.

BLAM

EUTIMIO GUERRA'S POWERS OF PREDICTION, ONCE AGAIN, WERE PROVEN ACCURATE.

CHE CHECKED HIS RESPIRATION, THEN HIS PULSE. BOTH WERE NORMAL.

JUST THEN A THUNDERSTORM BROKE.

BADOOM

HE THOUGHT OF JULIO ZENON, THE FIRST OF MANY PEASANTS THE REVOLUTION WOULD FREE FROM THE CHAINS OF ILLITERACY.

THE CLANDESTINE MOVEMENT IN THE CITIES BEGAN TO STIR.

JOVEN REBELDE
INSURGENTS LAND IN ORIENTE
POLICE STATION BLOWN UP

SOMETIMES CHE WAS SLOWED DOWN BY HIS ASTHMA.

PANT PUFF

GET UP THERE, YOU ARGENTINIAN ©!!♫?✳

BUT CASTRO ARRANGED FOR HIM TO BE LOOKED AFTER BY SYMPATHETIC PEASANTS.

IN HAVANA, THE JULY 26 STUDENT MOVEMENT STAGED AN UNSUCCESSFUL ATTACK ON THE PRESIDENTIAL PALACE.

AND IN THE MOUNTAINS THERE WAS A CHANGE IN THE ENEMY.

BRAP BDAM POOM PPAM
PTOW TATATAT

THEY'RE JUST SHOOTING INTO THE TREES BUT NO ONE'S THERE.

AND NONE OF THEM WANTS TO GO IN.

BECAUSE OF HIS OVERALL PERFORMANCE FIDEL GAVE CHE COMMAND RESPONSIBILITIES DESPITE HIS HEALTH PROBLEMS.

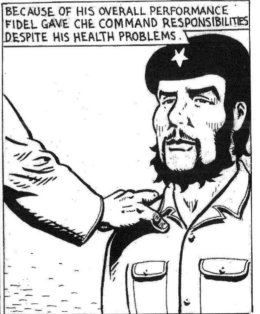

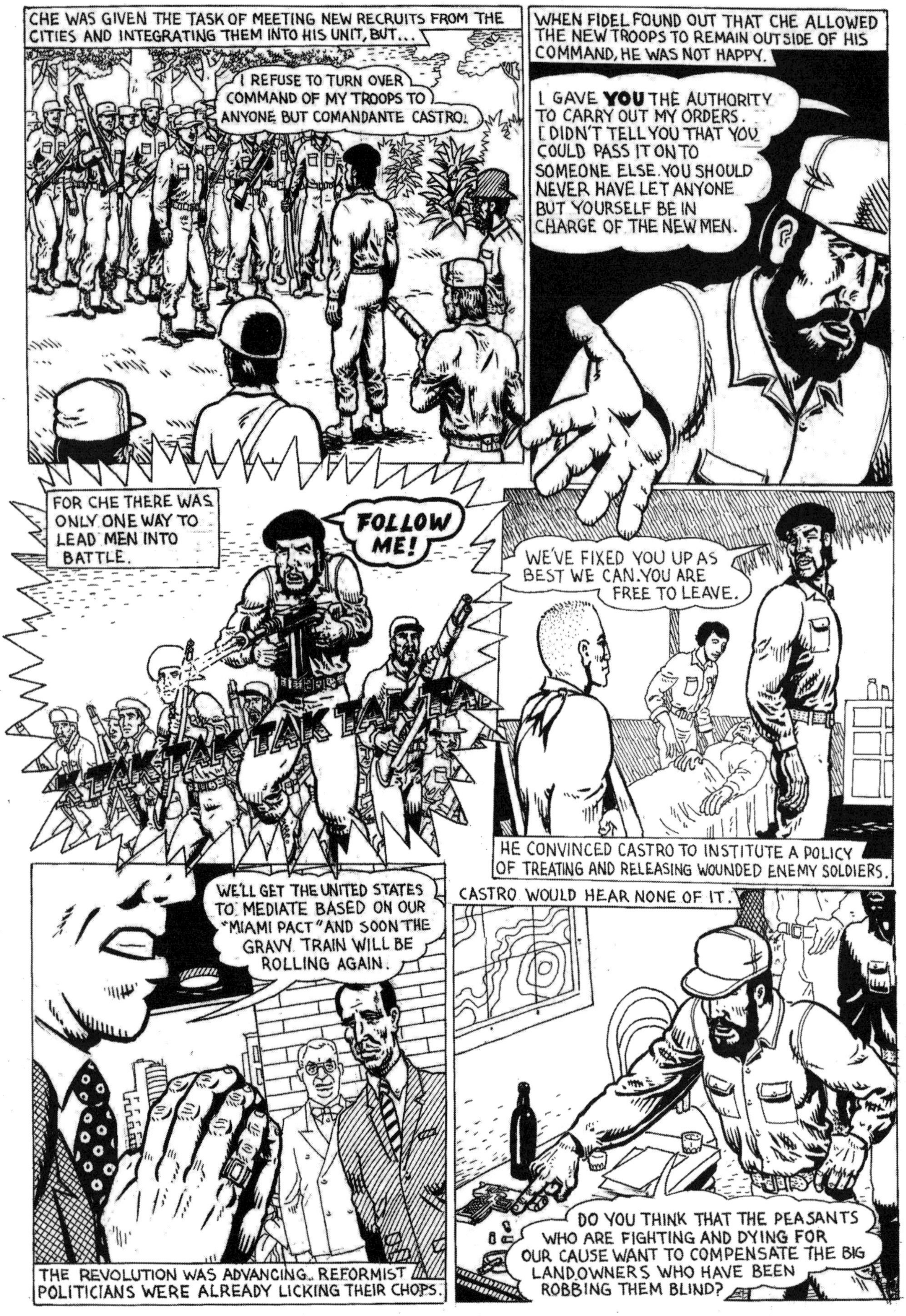
CHE WAS GIVEN THE TASK OF MEETING NEW RECRUITS FROM THE CITIES AND INTEGRATING THEM INTO HIS UNIT, BUT...
I REFUSE TO TURN OVER COMMAND OF MY TROOPS TO ANYONE BUT COMANDANTE CASTRO.
WHEN FIDEL FOUND OUT THAT CHE ALLOWED THE NEW TROOPS TO REMAIN OUTSIDE OF HIS COMMAND, HE WAS NOT HAPPY.
I GAVE YOU THE AUTHORITY TO CARRY OUT MY ORDERS. I DIDN'T TELL YOU THAT YOU COULD PASS IT ON TO SOMEONE ELSE. YOU SHOULD NEVER HAVE LET ANYONE BUT YOURSELF BE IN CHARGE OF THE NEW MEN.
FOR CHE THERE WAS ONLY ONE WAY TO LEAD MEN INTO BATTLE.
FOLLOW ME!
TAK TAK TAK TAK TAK
WE'VE FIXED YOU UP AS BEST WE CAN. YOU ARE FREE TO LEAVE.
HE CONVINCED CASTRO TO INSTITUTE A POLICY OF TREATING AND RELEASING WOUNDED ENEMY SOLDIERS.
WE'LL GET THE UNITED STATES TO MEDIATE BASED ON OUR "MIAMI PACT" AND SOON THE GRAVY TRAIN WILL BE ROLLING AGAIN.
THE REVOLUTION WAS ADVANCING... REFORMIST POLITICIANS WERE ALREADY LICKING THEIR CHOPS.
CASTRO WOULD HEAR NONE OF IT.
DO YOU THINK THAT THE PEASANTS WHO ARE FIGHTING AND DYING FOR OUR CAUSE WANT TO COMPENSATE THE BIG LANDOWNERS WHO HAVE BEEN ROBBING THEM BLIND?

CHE'S TREATMENT OF PRISONERS BORE TANGIBLE RESULTS WHEN ONE SOLDIER GAVE THEM A CODE BOOK AND RADIO TRANSMITTER.

THEY PUT BOTH TO GOOD USE, CALLING IN ENEMY AIR STRIKES ON THEIR OWN POSITIONS.

FIDEL ADAPTED AND REFINED CHE'S IDEAS. THE REBELS WERE STARTING TO HOLD TERRITORY.

THE FIRST SCHOOLS AND HOSPITALS IN THE REGION WERE BUILT IN LIBERATED AREAS. THEY ALSO BUILT FACTORIES THAT TURNED OUT UNIFORMS.

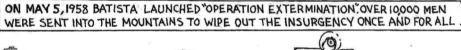

ON MAY 5, 1958 BATISTA LAUNCHED "OPERATION EXTERMINATION". OVER 10,000 MEN WERE SENT INTO THE MOUNTAINS TO WIPE OUT THE INSURGENCY ONCE AND FOR ALL.

FIDEL CASTRO DEFTLY MANEUVERED HIS VASTLY OUTNUMBERED FORCES.

THEN AS YOU FALL BACK TO LA MOSQUERA, CAMILO WILL ATTACK FROM HERE.

PHEW!

MOVING IN UNFAMILIAR TERRAIN, BATISTA'S MEN WERE NOT PREPARED FOR THE RIGORS OF MOUNTAIN WARFARE.

BLAM

POOM

PTAK

CHE'S COLUMN HELPED REPULSE GOVERNMENT ATTACKS IN JULY AT EL JIGÜE AND SANTO DOMINGO.

POOM BAM PLAK BLAM TOK PAK TAK TAK TAK KBOOM POP

THE REBELS STRUCK HARD AT THE TIME AND PLACE OF THEIR OWN CHOOSING.

GOVERNMENT FORCES FLED IN DISARRAY. THE REBELS CAPTURED 12 MORTARS, 12 MACHINE GUNS, 500 MODERN RIFLES AND PLENTY OF MUCH-NEEDED AMMUNITION.

THEY EVEN CAPTURED A TANK.

APPEALS WERE MADE TO THE AMERICAN EMBASSY ABOUT STOPPING MATERIAL SENT TO BATISTA.

IF YOU LOOK CLOSELY AT THE WORDING OF THE TREATY, IT SAYS MILITARY COOPERATION IS "SUBJECT TO CANCELLATION IN CASES OF CIVIL UNREST." I.E.; IT "MAY" BE SUBJECT TO CANCELLATION, ON THE OTHER HAND, IT MAY NOT.

THE U.S. CONTINUED TO SUPPLY ARMS TO THE DICTATOR UNTIL HE FLED THE COUNTRY.

MANY WOMEN IN THE CAMP HAD THEIR EYE ON CHE, BUT ONE WOMAN CAUGHT HIS ATTENTION.

HIS BEAUTIFUL BLACK COMPANION WAS SOON HELPING HIM EASE THE HARSHNESS OF CAMP LIFE.

BUT CHE'S ROMANTIC INTERLUDE WAS INTERRUPTED BY FIDEL.

IT'S TIME TO MOVE OUR FORCES INTO THE CENTER OF THE COUNTRY.

CAMILO CIENFUEGOS, CHE GUEVARA AND MY BROTHER, RAUL, WILL MOVE THEIR MEN TO THE ESCAMBRAY MOUNTAINS.

CHE'S COLUMN ADVANCED TO THE ESCAMBRAY UNDER HURRICANE-LIKE CONDITIONS.

WHEN THE RAINS STOPPED, THE BOMBING BEGAN.

SOMEHOW HE MANAGED TO GET HIS TROOPS, MANY OF THEM NEW RECRUITS, TO THE MOUNTAINS WITH ONLY A FEW CASUALTIES.

OVER THE OBJECTIONS OF SOME URBAN MEMBERS OF THE JULY 26 MOVEMENT, CHE INSTITUTED LAND REFORM IN NEWLY LIBERATED ZONES.

POLICE IN THESE AREAS WERE GLAD TO SURRENDER TO THE REBELS, FEARING THE WRATH OF PEOPLE THEY HAD BULLIED AND TORTURED.

INSURGENT SABOTAGE AND GENERAL INDIFFERENCE THWARTED BATISTA'S ATTEMPT TO PULL OFF A SHAM ELECTION.

THE NEXT ATTACK WAS ON SANTA CLARA, THE CAPITAL OF LAS VILLAS PROVINCE, BUT ONCE THEY ENTERED THE CITY THEY FOUND THAT THE INHABITANTS HAD ALREADY ERECTED BARRICADES.

EVEN THOUGH THEY OUTNUMBERED CHE'S FORCES BY MORE THAN TEN TO ONE, THE SOLDIERS REMAINED HOLED-UP IN THEIR BARRACKS.

BUT THEN...

COMANDANTE, WE HAVE JUST GOTTEN WORD THAT AN ARMORED TRAIN FILLED WITH REINFORCEMENTS IS COMING FROM CAMAJUANI!

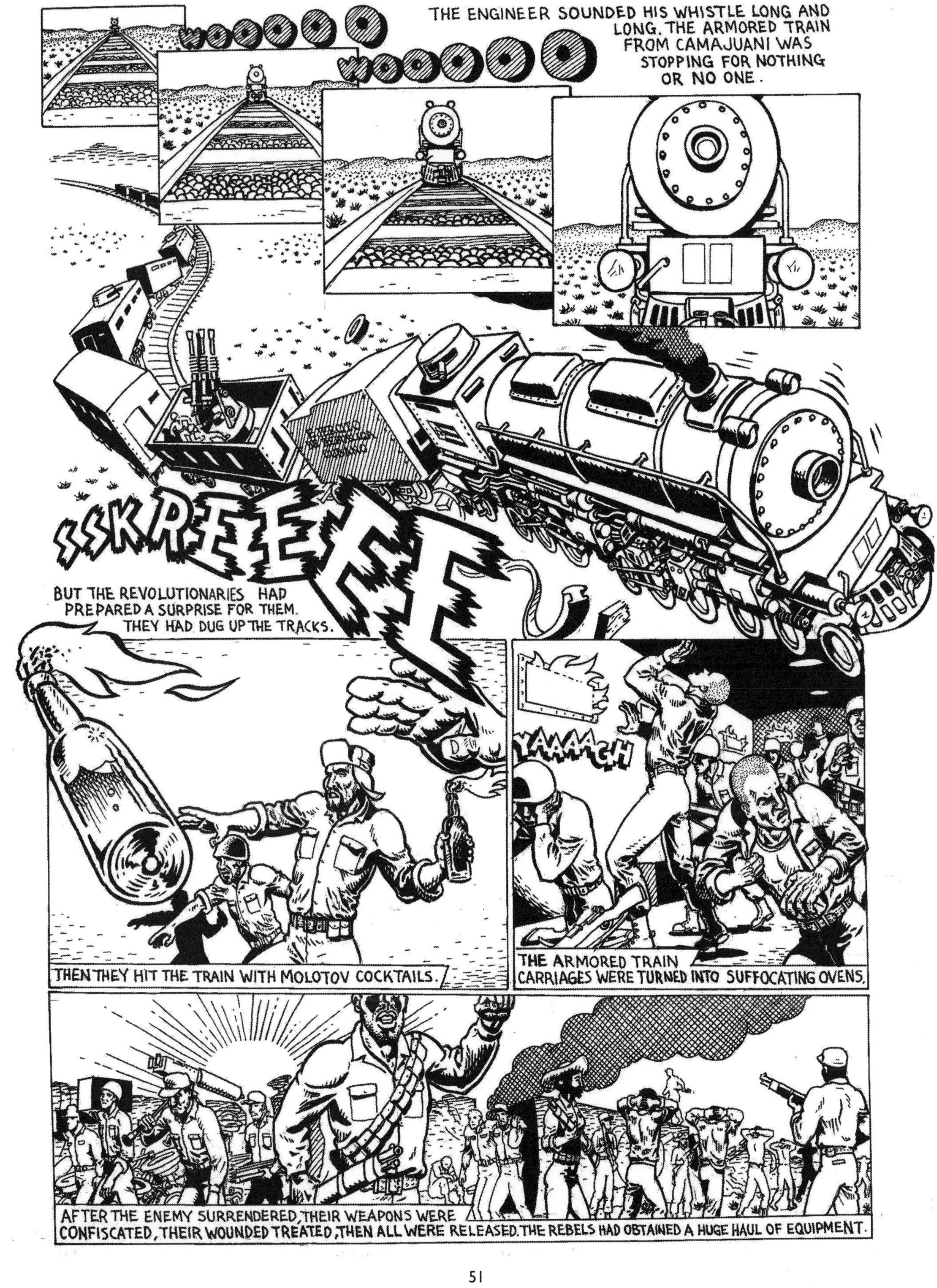
WOOOOO
WOOOOO
THE ENGINEER SOUNDED HIS WHISTLE LONG AND LONG. THE ARMORED TRAIN FROM CAMAJUANI WAS STOPPING FOR NOTHING OR NO ONE.
SSKREEFF
BUT THE REVOLUTIONARIES HAD PREPARED A SURPRISE FOR THEM. THEY HAD DUG UP THE TRACKS.
THEN THEY HIT THE TRAIN WITH MOLOTOV COCKTAILS.
YAAAACH
THE ARMORED TRAIN CARRIAGES WERE TURNED INTO SUFFOCATING OVENS.
AFTER THE ENEMY SURRENDERED, THEIR WEAPONS WERE CONFISCATED, THEIR WOUNDED TREATED, THEN ALL WERE RELEASED. THE REBELS HAD OBTAINED A HUGE HAUL OF EQUIPMENT.

GOVERNMENT BOMBING OF CIVILIAN AREAS DID NOT PREVENT THE SURRENDER OF THE SANTA CLARA GARRISON, ADDING TO THE REBELS' SUPPLY OF EQUIPMENT.

IN THE MEANTIME FIDEL HAD TAKEN THE EASTERN CITY OF SANTIAGO.

FIDEL WANTS YOU TO MOVE YOUR TROOPS INTO HAVANA.

TELL HIM I'M ON MY WAY!

30 CAL.

GENERAL FULGENCIO BATISTA FLED THE COUNTRY AT 2:10 A.M. NEW YEARS DAY 1959.

BUT BATISTA HAD ONE LAST TRICK UP HIS SLEEVE. HE APPOINTED ONE OF HIS GENERALS, CANTILLO, AS HEAD OF STATE.

WE ARE NOW THE LEGITIMATE GOVERNMENT OF CUBA. ANY NEGOTIATIONS ON CUBA'S FUTURE WILL HAVE TO DEAL DIRECTLY WITH US.

HOWEVER...

THERE'S NOTHING TO NEGOTIATE. OUR TROOPS ARE ALREADY IN HAVANA.

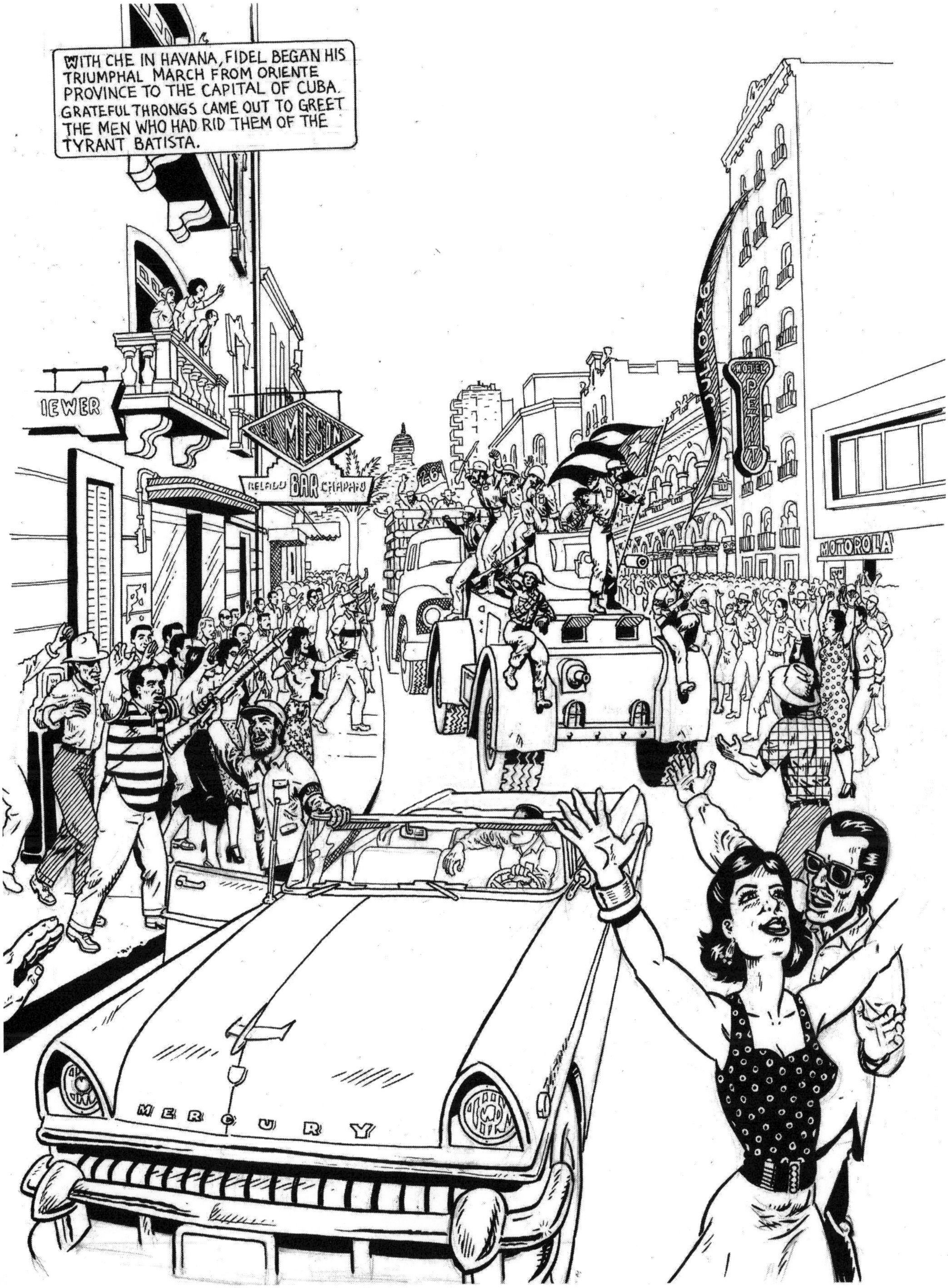
WITH CHE IN HAVANA, FIDEL BEGAN HIS TRIUMPHAL MARCH FROM ORIENTE PROVINCE TO THE CAPITAL OF CUBA. GRATEFUL THRONGS CAME OUT TO GREET THE MEN WHO HAD RID THEM OF THE TYRANT BATISTA.
IEWER
BAR
MOTOROLA
MERCURY

AS SMALL POCKETS OF BATISTA HOLDOUTS WERE MOPPED UP, IT WAS THE FIRST TIME IN LATIN AMERICAN HISTORY THAT AN ARMY SURRENDERED TO ITS PEOPLE.

PERHAPS IT WAS WISHFUL THINKING THAT PROMPTED HEADLINES IN U.S. PAPERS, BUT...

Des Moines Express

BATISTA CRUSHES INSURGENTS

REVOLT OVER, SAYS UNNAMED GOVERNMENT SOURCE

SENATOR KENNEDY PROPOSES NEW MEASURES

MINE DISASTER IN OHIO

THE TORTURERS NOW HAD GOOD REASON TO FEAR THE PEOPLE'S THIRST FOR REVENGE.

HOW WOULD YOU LIKE A DOSE OF YOUR OWN MEDICINE, RAT?

CASTRO WORKED TO HEAD OFF A BLOOD BATH.

WE ARE NOT LIKE THEM. WE ARE REVOLUTIONARIES AND MUST LIVE UP TO A HIGHER STANDARD. THE CRIMINALS OF THE OLD REGIME WILL BE TRIED AND BROUGHT TO JUSTICE.

THIS DID NOT DETER PEOPLE FROM DEMOLISHING BATISTA'S DUNGEONS AND TORTURE CHAMBERS.

BA-BOOM

...THEN HE TOLD HIS MEN TO DRAG WHAT WAS LEFT OF THEIR BODIES INTO THE JUNGLE AND LEAVE THEM THERE.

IN TRIALS OPEN TO THE PUBLIC, MOST OF THE ACCUSED WERE FOUND GUILTY ON THE DETAILED TESTIMONY OF EYEWITNESSES.

GUEVARA WAS PUT IN CHARGE OF LA CABAÑA FORTRESS, WHERE THE TORMENTORS OF THE CUBAN PEOPLE MET SWIFT JUSTICE.

THE SPATE OF BLOODLETTING CONTINUES IN CUBA...

SUDDENLY THE AMERICAN MEDIA, WHICH HADN'T LET OUT A PEEP WHEN OVER 20,000 COMMON PEOPLE WERE MURDERED, BEGAN TO WAX INDIGNANT.

CHE HAD INJURED HIS WRIST DURING THE BRIEF FIGHTING ENTERING HAVANA, AND WAS NOT VERY COMFORTABLE DURING HIS FIRST INTERVIEW.

TO LABEL "COMMUNISTS" ALL THOSE WHO REFUSE TO BOW DOWN IS AN OLD DICTATOR'S TRICK.

REPORTERS THEN SPOKE TO ONE OF HIS STAFF, ALEIDA MARCH.

I CAN'T SAY I'M CHE'S SECRETARY BECAUSE I'M A FIGHTER. I FOUGHT BESIDE HIM IN THE LAS VILLAS CAMPAIGN. THAT MAKES ME HIS ORDERLY.

ALEIDA MARCH WAS IN THE CLANDESTINE WING OF THE JULY 26 MOVEMENT. HER WORK IN SANTA CLARA BECAME TOO DANGEROUS AND SHE HAD TO FLEE TO THE ESCAMBRAY MOUNTAINS WHERE SHE AND CHE MET AND FELL IN LOVE. LATER THEY WOULD MARRY.

WHEN HIS WIFE, HILDA, ARRIVED, CHE CONVEYED NEWS OF HIS NEW LOVE TO HER.

BETTER I HAD DIED IN COMBAT.

THE INSURGENTS WERE MOSTLY A PEASANT ARMY WHO HAD NEVER BEFORE GLIMPSED HAVANA NIGHT LIFE.

AT THE TIME HAVANA WAS A CENTER OF EROTIC ENTERTAINMENT. A PERFORMER CALLED "SUPERMAN" THRILLED AUDIENCES NIGHTLY.

A FAVORITE SPOT FOR MAKING LOVE WAS IN THE BUSHES BENEATH THE STATUE OF JESUS CHRIST.

NUESTRO BENDIGO SEÑIOR JESUS CHRISTO

IN AN EFFORT TO CURB THE EPIDEMIC OF HI-JINKS, CHE INSTITUTED MASS MARRIAGE CEREMONIES (SECULAR OR RELIGIOUS) FOR THOSE WHO DESIRED THEM.

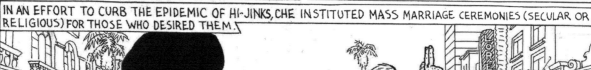

FINALLY, EXHAUSTED AND FIGHTING OFF ANOTHER BOUT OF ASTHMA, CHE RETREATED TO A HOUSE IN TARARÁ, NEAR THE SEA.

WHEN PRESIDENT URRUTIA RETURNED FROM EXILE CHE AND FIDEL WERE ON HAND TO GREET HIM.

ALTHOUGH URRUTIA OCCUPIED THE PRESIDENTIAL PALACE FIDEL CALLED THE SHOTS. HE APPOINTED A PRO-BUSINESS CABINET, INCLUDING ANTI-COMMUNISTS.

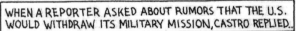

WHEN A REPORTER ASKED ABOUT RUMORS THAT THE U.S. WOULD WITHDRAW ITS MILITARY MISSION, CASTRO REPLIED.

THEY HAVE TO WITHDRAW. THE UNITED STATES HAS NO RIGHT TO A PERMANENT MISSION HERE. THIS DECISION IS ONLY THE PREROGATIVE OF THE REVOLUTIONARY GOVERNMENT OF CUBA.

WELCOME!

CAMILO CIENFUEGOS WAS ASSIGNED TO MEET THE U.S. AMBASSADOR. IT APPEARED THAT CHE HAD BEEN SIDELINED.

BUT IN THE HOUSE BY THE SEA AT TARARA', MEETINGS WENT ON TILL EARLY MORNING.

THE FAILURE OF ARBENZ TO CONFRONT GUATEMALA'S SECURITY LED TO HIS OVERTHROW.

THERE CHE AND CASTRO'S BROTHER, RAUL, MET WITH MEMBERS OF THE P.S.P. (THE CUBAN COMMUNIST PARTY.)

CHE INITIALLY WAS NOT VERY IMPRESSED WITH THE P.S.P.

THE COMMUNISTS ARE ABLE TO TRAIN CADRES WHO LET THEMSELVE BE RIPPED TO SHREDS IN A DARK DUNGEON WITHOUT A WORD, BUT NOT CADRES WHO WILL TAKE A MACHINE-GUN NEST BY STORM.

WE CONDEMN THE "PUTSCH" METHODS TYPICAL OF BOURGEOIS FACTIONS USED IN THE SANTIAGO RAID. THE HEROISM DISPLAYED BY THE PARTICIPANTS' ACTION IS FALSE AND STERILE.

EVEN THOUGH THEY HAD BEEN DRIVEN UNDERGROUND BY BATISTA, THE PARTY DIDN'T HAVE MUCH USE FOR THE JULY 26 MOVEMENT EITHER. THEY HAD CONDEMNED THE ATTACK ON THE MONCADA BARRACKS.

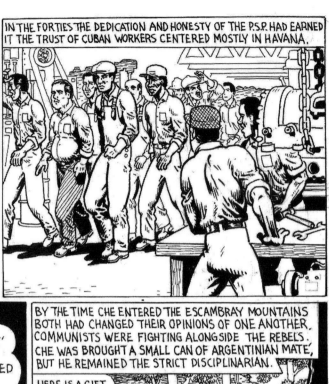

IN THE FORTIES THE DEDICATION AND HONESTY OF THE P.S.P. HAD EARNED IT THE TRUST OF CUBAN WORKERS CENTERED MOSTLY IN HAVANA.

BY THE TIME CHE ENTERED THE ESCAMBRAY MOUNTAINS BOTH HAD CHANGED THEIR OPINIONS OF ONE ANOTHER. COMMUNISTS WERE FIGHTING ALONGSIDE THE REBELS. CHE WAS BROUGHT A SMALL CAN OF ARGENTINIAN MATE', BUT HE REMAINED THE STRICT DISCIPLINARIAN.

HERE IS A GIFT FROM PARTY LEADERSHIP.

THANK YOU. BUT TELL THEM NOT TO SEND ANY MORE GIFTS.

THIS LAND THAT YOU'VE WORKED ON FOR YEARS, NOW BELONGS TO YOU.

HOW ABOUT THE OXEN?

TAKE THEM TOO.

BUT MOST IMPORTANTLY THEY SUPPORTED CHE'S IDEAS ON LAND REFORM.

CONTRARY TO GUEVARA'S EXPECTATIONS, THE RECRUITS THAT THE PARTY SENT PROVED TO BE EFFECTIVE FIGHTERS.

AT HUGE OUTDOOR RALLIES FIDEL PROMULGATED HIS IDEAS OF "DIRECT DEMOCRACY" TO HIS RECEPTIVE COUNTRYMEN.

AT SOME POINT DURING THE FIRST EVENT, DOVES RELEASED FROM THE AUDIENCE CAME TO REST ON CASTRO'S SHOULDERS. THIS PIECE OF SPONTANEOUS THEATRICS DID NOTHING TO DIMINISH THE SENSE OF HIS CONNECTION TO THE CUBAN PEOPLE.

CHEERING CROWDS GREETED CHE AND FIDEL WHEN THEY TOURED LATIN AMERICA THAT APRIL. IN THE U.S. EVEN THE STATE DEPT. WAS CORDIAL.

BUT THE EISENHOWER ADMINISTRATION WAS DISTURBED BY REPORTS OF "COMMUNIST INDOCTRINATION" IN THE EDUCATIONAL PROGRAMS CHE HAD BEGUN AT LA CABAÑA.

AFTER AN AMICABLE DIVORCE FROM HILDA, CHE AND ALEIDA WERE MARRIED ON JUNE 2, 1959.

PRESIDENT URRUTIA CLOSED DOWN THE CASINOS. BY JULY HE HAD LEFT OFFICE.

THE REVOLUTIONARY GOVERNMENT LOWERED PHONE AND ELECTRICITY RATES. RENTS WERE ROLLED BACK.

REDUCCION DE LAS RENTAS

BUT NOT EVERYONE WAS PLEASED WITH THE POLICIES OF THE NEW GOVERNMENT.

LAND REFORM! WE'LL SEE ABOUT THAT...

CHE WAS INVITED BY PRESIDENT NASSER TO VISIT EGYPT.

SOME SPECULATED THAT CASTRO WANTED TO GET CHE OUT OF SIGHT WHILE HE MOVED THE GOVERNMENT IN A MORE MODERATE DIRECTION.

ON A TOUR OF THE PYRAMIDS NASSER TALKED ABOUT RECENT EVENTS.

...SO AFTER THE BRITISH REFUSED TO PURCHASE EGYPTIAN COTTON, I SOLD THE WHOLE CROP TO THE SOVIET BLOCK.

HMMM!

CHE TRAVELED TO THE THIRD WORLD SETTING UP TRADE AGREEMENTS AS A REPRESENTATIVE OF I.N.R.A., THE CUBAN AGRARIAN MINISTRY.

MANY OF THESE COUNTRIES WOULD LATER BECOME MEMBERS OF THE CONGRESS OF NON-ALIGNED NATIONS.

UPON HIS RETURN IN SEPTEMBER HE WAS MADE HEAD OF THE CUBAN NATIONAL BANK. HIS STYE WAS CHARACTERISTICALLY INFORMAL YET EFFICIENT AND DISCIPLINED.

NOW MEASURES WERE TAKEN TO PROVIDE HEALTH CARE IN RURAL AREAS, AND SCHOOLS WERE BUILT IN PLACES THAT NEVER HAD SCHOOLS BEFORE.

THE DAYS OF PRIVILEGE WERE OVER FOR CUBA'S RULING CLASS.

IN EARLY 1960 CHE WAS VISITED BY FRENCH PHILOSOPHERS, JEAN PAUL SARTRE AND SIMONE DE BEAUVOIR.

NO MATTER HOW IMPORTANT NATURAL FACTORS ARE, THE EVIL THAT AFFLICTS MANKIND COMES FROM OTHER MEN.

SOON THE WELL-OFF WERE LEAVING THE COUNTRY TO JOIN THE REMNANTS OF BATISTA SUPPORTERS IN MIAMI.

THE LAST MODERATE POLITICIANS LEFT THE GOVERNMENT WHEN CASTRO BEGAN A PROGRAM OF NATIONALIZATION OF THE SUGAR MILLS AND OTHER INDUSTRIES, TURNING SOME INTO COOPERATIVES.

ON MAY DAY 1960 CUBA'S SOVIET-SUPPLIED MILITARY WAS ON DISPLAY. NOW THE U.S. HAD TO CONTEND WITH A WELL-ARMED PEASANT ARMY READY TO DEFEND ITS GAINS.

BUT THE UNITED STATES HAD OTHER MEANS TO MAKE ITS DISPLEASURE FELT.

SLAM

NO MORE OIL FOR CUBA!

BUT OIL WAS FORTHCOMING... FROM THE SOVIET UNION.

HOWEVER...

NO! WE WILL NOT REFINE SOVIET OIL.

THEN WE'LL JUST HAVE TO NATIONALIZE YOUR REFINERY.

DON'T BE RIDICULOUS, IT'S BEYOND YOUR ABILITY TO OPERATE.

THE TELEPHONE AND ELECTRIC COMPANIES OWNED BY U.S. CITIZENS HAD BEEN NATIONALIZED. NOW CUBA TOOK OVER THE REFINERIES. ALL TECHNICAL DIFFICULTIES WERE OVERCOME. CUBA'S INDEPENDENCE HAD ADVANCED.

CUBAN FINANCIAL RESERVES HAD DROPPED FROM $75 MILLION TO $50 MILLION. WITH CHE AT THE HELM, BY THE TIME OF THE SOVIET TRADE EXHIBITION IN HAVANA IN FEBRUARY, IT HAD RISEN TO $65 MILLION. IN A FEW MONTHS IT WOULD RISE TO $150 MILLION. SOVIET OIL WAS SOON TO BE TRADED FOR SUGAR.

A NEWSPAPER OFFICE WAS WRECKED WHEN IT CALLED CASTRO "THE ANTI-CHRIST." OTHER OPPOSITION PAPERS WERE SOON CLOSED DOWN. THERE WAS NO LONGER FREEDOM IN CUBA FOR THOSE WHO OWNED THE PRESSES.

IN JULY 1960, THE WAR OF WORDS ESCALATED AS PRESIDENT EISENHOWER PROCLAIMED...

THE UNITED STATES WILL NOT PERMIT A REGIME DOMINATED BY INTERNATIONAL COMMUNISM IN CUBA.

MANY AMERICANS WERE GENUINELY PERPLEXED BY CUBA'S ATTITUDE.

I DON'T UNDERSTAND THEM. FOR SIX MONTHS OF THE YEAR CUBAN MEN CAN RELAX WHILE THEIR WOMEN SERVICE AMERICAN TOURISTS; THEY ONLY HAVE TO WORK HALF A YEAR. THEY GOT IT MADE!

AND IN MIAMI, THE EXILES REJOICED IN THEIR ANTICIPATED RETURN.

I KNEW THE NORTH AMERICANS WOULDN'T PUT UP WITH THIS NONSENSE

SOON WE'LL BE BACK IN POWER.

DEATH TO THE COMMUNISTS!

SOON DISAFFECTED REVOLUTIONARIES JOINED BATISTA HOLD-OUTS IN THE ESCAMBRAY MOUNTAINS. CIA FUNDS FLOWED FREELY.

IN OTHER PARTS OF THE COUNTRY NEW HOUSING WAS REPLACING PEASANTS' SHACKS.

WHEN CHE WAS VISITING AMERICA, VICE-PRESIDENT RICHARD NIXON HAD LAID OUT WHAT WAS EXPECTED BY THE U.S.

NOW THAT YOU HAVE POWER YOU MUST ACT RESPONSIBLY. YOU CAN'T NECESSARILY GIVE THE PEOPLE WHAT THEY WANT.

AS LITERACY WORKERS WERE GUNNED DOWN IN RURAL AREAS, CUBA SAW THE CONSEQUENCES OF FAILING TO MEET AMERICAN EXPECTATIONS.

BUT THE COUNTER-REVOLUTIONARIES COULD GARNER LITTLE SUPPORT FROM POOR PEASANTS WHO REMAINED FAITHFUL TO THE REVOLUTION.

THAT'S RIGHT! ABOUT TWENTY OF THEM CAME BY HERE THREE DAYS AGO.

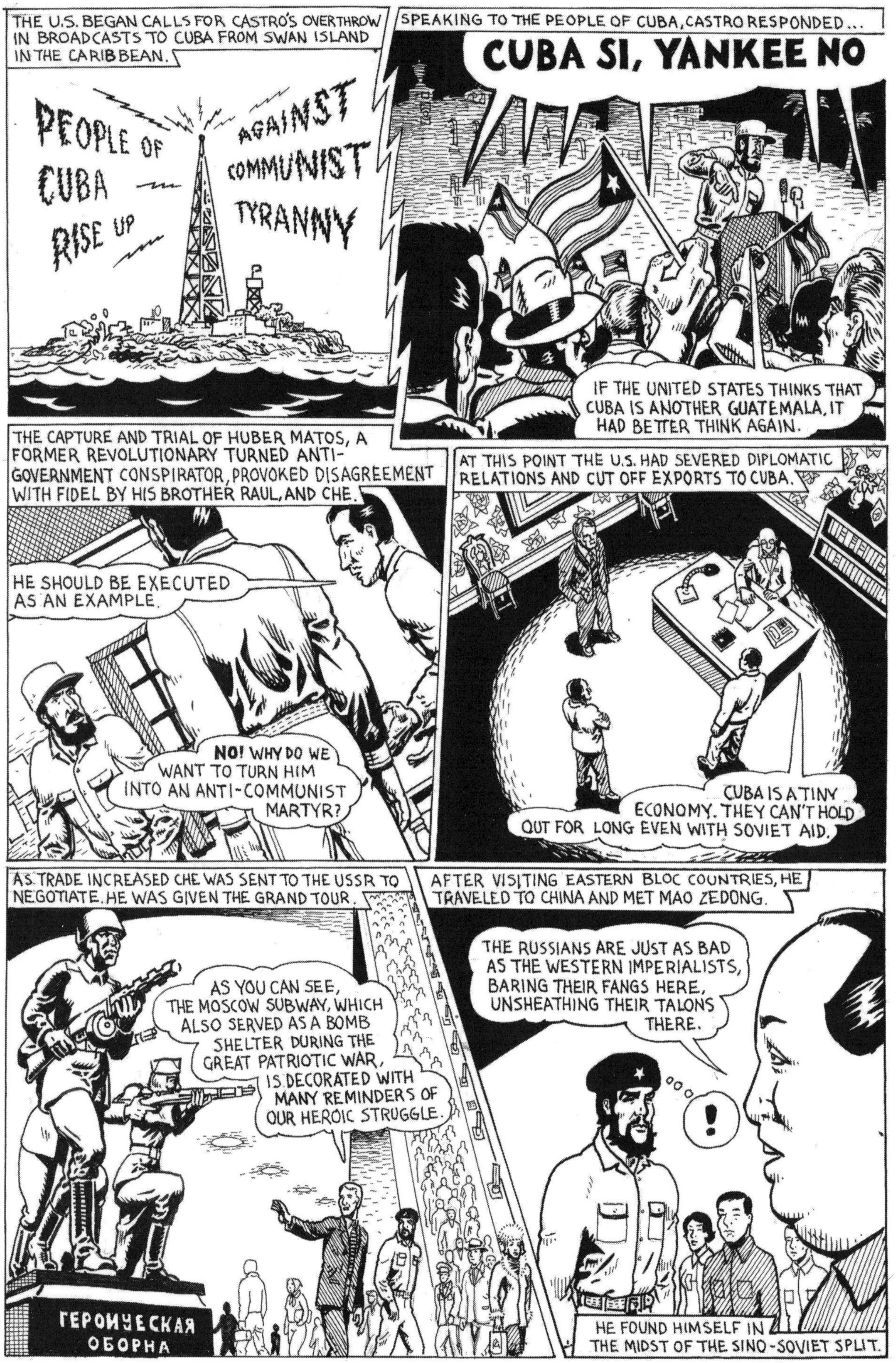
THE U.S. BEGAN CALLS FOR CASTRO'S OVERTHROW IN BROADCASTS TO CUBA FROM SWAN ISLAND IN THE CARIBBEAN.
PEOPLE OF CUBA RISE UP AGAINST COMMUNIST TYRANNY
SPEAKING TO THE PEOPLE OF CUBA, CASTRO RESPONDED...
CUBA SI, YANKEE NO
IF THE UNITED STATES THINKS THAT CUBA IS ANOTHER GUATEMALA, IT HAD BETTER THINK AGAIN.
THE CAPTURE AND TRIAL OF HUBER MATOS, A FORMER REVOLUTIONARY TURNED ANTI-GOVERNMENT CONSPIRATOR, PROVOKED DISAGREEMENT WITH FIDEL BY HIS BROTHER RAUL, AND CHE.
HE SHOULD BE EXECUTED AS AN EXAMPLE.
NO! WHY DO WE WANT TO TURN HIM INTO AN ANTI-COMMUNIST MARTYR?
AT THIS POINT THE U.S. HAD SEVERED DIPLOMATIC RELATIONS AND CUT OFF EXPORTS TO CUBA.
CUBA IS A TINY ECONOMY. THEY CAN'T HOLD OUT FOR LONG EVEN WITH SOVIET AID.
AS TRADE INCREASED CHE WAS SENT TO THE USSR TO NEGOTIATE. HE WAS GIVEN THE GRAND TOUR.
AS YOU CAN SEE, THE MOSCOW SUBWAY, WHICH ALSO SERVED AS A BOMB SHELTER DURING THE GREAT PATRIOTIC WAR, IS DECORATED WITH MANY REMINDERS OF OUR HEROIC STRUGGLE.
ГЕРОИЧЕСКАЯ ОБОРНА
AFTER VISITING EASTERN BLOC COUNTRIES, HE TRAVELED TO CHINA AND MET MAO ZEDONG.
THE RUSSIANS ARE JUST AS BAD AS THE WESTERN IMPERIALISTS, BARING THEIR FANGS HERE, UNSHEATHING THEIR TALONS THERE.
!
HE FOUND HIMSELF IN THE MIDST OF THE SINO-SOVIET SPLIT.

IN FACT, THE CUBAN REVOLUTION HAD MUCH IN COMMON WITH THE CHINESE REVOLUTION. BOTH WERE MADE BY ARMIES OF PEASANTS WHO HAD BEEN WON OVER BY FAIR TREATMENT.

BUT PRACTICAL CONSIDERATIONS DICTATED ALIGNMENT WITH THE USSR AND ITS ALLIES.

A PLANE FLYING FROM MIAMI DROPPED LEAFLETS OVER HAVANA CALLING ON CUBANS TO OUST FIDEL CASTRO.

FUERA CASTRO
FUERA CASTRO DEL PUEBLO DE CUBA

FIDEL'S "WATCHERS" IN MIAMI NOTICED CIA RECRUITMENT DRIVES WERE BEING STEPPED UP.

BRIGADE 2506

MEANWHILE, EXCLUSIVE BEACHES WERE OPENED TO ORDINARY CUBANS FOR THE FIRST TIME.

IN THE EARLY MONTHS OF VICTORY IN CUBA, UNSUCCESSFUL ATTEMPTS WERE MADE TO OVERTHROW CARIBBEAN DICTATORS SUCH AS NICARAGUA'S SOMOZA.

NOW IT WAS PAYBACK TIME.

EISENHOWER PASSED OFF THE PLAN TO INVADE CUBA ON TO THE INCOMING KENNEDY ADMINISTRATION.

OUR REPORTS SHOW THAT CUBANS ARE FED UP WITH CASTRO. WE'LL BE GREETED AS LIBERATORS IN THE STREETS OF HAVANA.

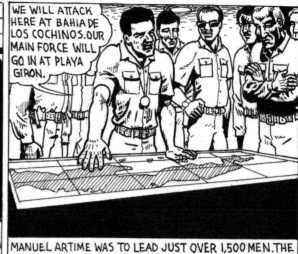

WE WILL ATTACK HERE AT BAHIA DE LOS COCHINOS. OUR MAIN FORCE WILL GO IN AT PLAYA GIRON.

MANUEL ARTIME WAS TO LEAD JUST OVER 1,500 MEN. THE AREA WAS PICKED BECAUSE THE LOCAL POPULATION WAS THOUGHT TO BE SYMPATHETIC TO THE COUNTER-REVOLUTION.

THE CAMPAIGN BEGAN WITH THE BOMBING OF A DEPARTMENT STORE.

BRAK BRAK

VLOK

EIGHT B-26 BOMBERS TOOK OFF FROM NICARAGUA. ONLY SIX REACHED THE AIRFIELD AT SANTIAGO.

TWO PLANES DECIDED TO HEAD STRAIGHT TO FLORIDA. THE U.S. MEDIA LATER CLAIMED THEY HAD DEFECTED FROM THE CUBAN AIR FORCE.

ON THE 16TH OF APRIL 1961 THE MAIN INVASION FORCE CARRIED BY THE LAKE CHARLES, ATLANTICO, BLAGAR, HOUSTON AND THE RIO ESCONDIDO PLUS ASSORTED SURPLUS U.S. LANDING CRAFT MET 30 MILES OFF THE CUBAN COAST.

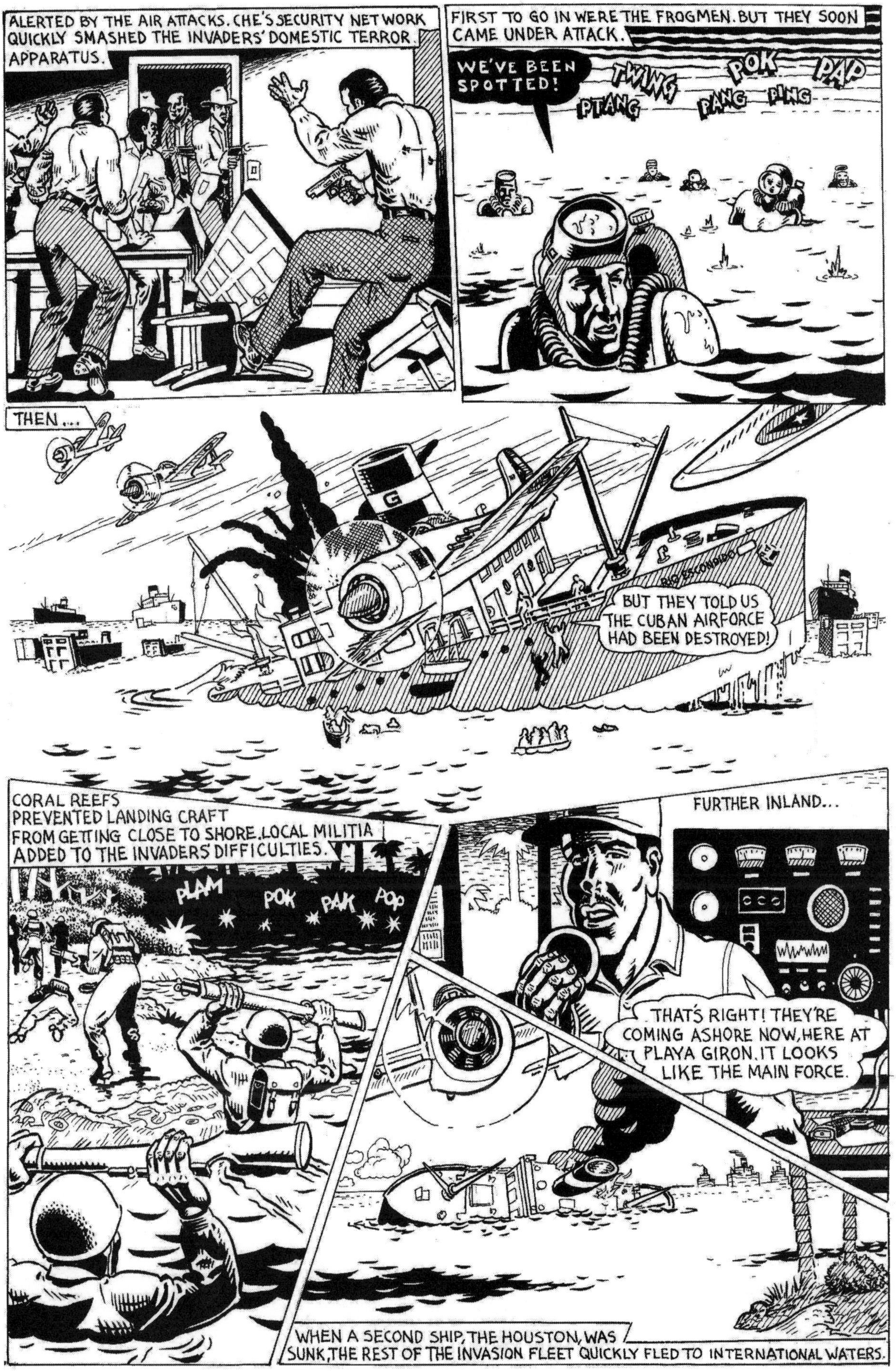
ALERTED BY THE AIR ATTACKS, CHE'S SECURITY NETWORK QUICKLY SMASHED THE INVADERS' DOMESTIC TERROR APPARATUS.
FIRST TO GO IN WERE THE FROGMEN. BUT THEY SOON CAME UNDER ATTACK.
WE'VE BEEN SPOTTED!
TWING
POK
PAP
PTANG
PANG
PING
THEN...
BUT THEY TOLD US THE CUBAN AIRFORCE HAD BEEN DESTROYED!
CORAL REEFS PREVENTED LANDING CRAFT FROM GETTING CLOSE TO SHORE. LOCAL MILITIA ADDED TO THE INVADERS' DIFFICULTIES.
PLAM
POK
PAK
POP
FURTHER INLAND...
THAT'S RIGHT! THEY'RE COMING ASHORE NOW, HERE AT PLAYA GIRON. IT LOOKS LIKE THE MAIN FORCE.
WHEN A SECOND SHIP, THE HOUSTON, WAS SUNK, THE REST OF THE INVASION FLEET QUICKLY FLED TO INTERNATIONAL WATERS.

WHEN SOME TANKS MADE IT ASHORE, THE INVADERS MANAGED TO CAPTURE GIRON TOWN.

MEANWHILE CASTRO MUSTERED HIS FORCES FOR THE COUNTER ATTACK.

THEY MUST BE PREVENTED FROM GAINING A FOOTHOLD. THEY PLAN TO DECLARE A PROVISIONAL GOVERNMENT AND INVITE THE U.S. TO INVADE.

THE 339th MILITIA BATTALION WAS FIRST DOWN THE NARROW CAUSEWAY TO GIRON.

BUT DROPPED IN BEHIND THEM WERE ENEMY PARATROOPERS.

IN GIRON, THE "FREEDOM FIGHTERS" SAVORED THEIR MOMENT OF VICTORY.

DID YOU THINK WE WOULD NOT BE BACK TO PUT AN END TO YOUR CRIMINAL ENTERPRISE?

PTUI

YOU OBVIOUSLY NEED TO LEARN SOME RESPECT FOR THE LAW!

SMAK SLAK

PIG! THE CUBAN PEOPLE ARE ON THEIR WAY AND THEY'RE COMING FOR THE LIKES OF YOU.

WE'LL SEE THE EXTENT OF YOUR BRAVERY WHEN THEY ARRIVE.

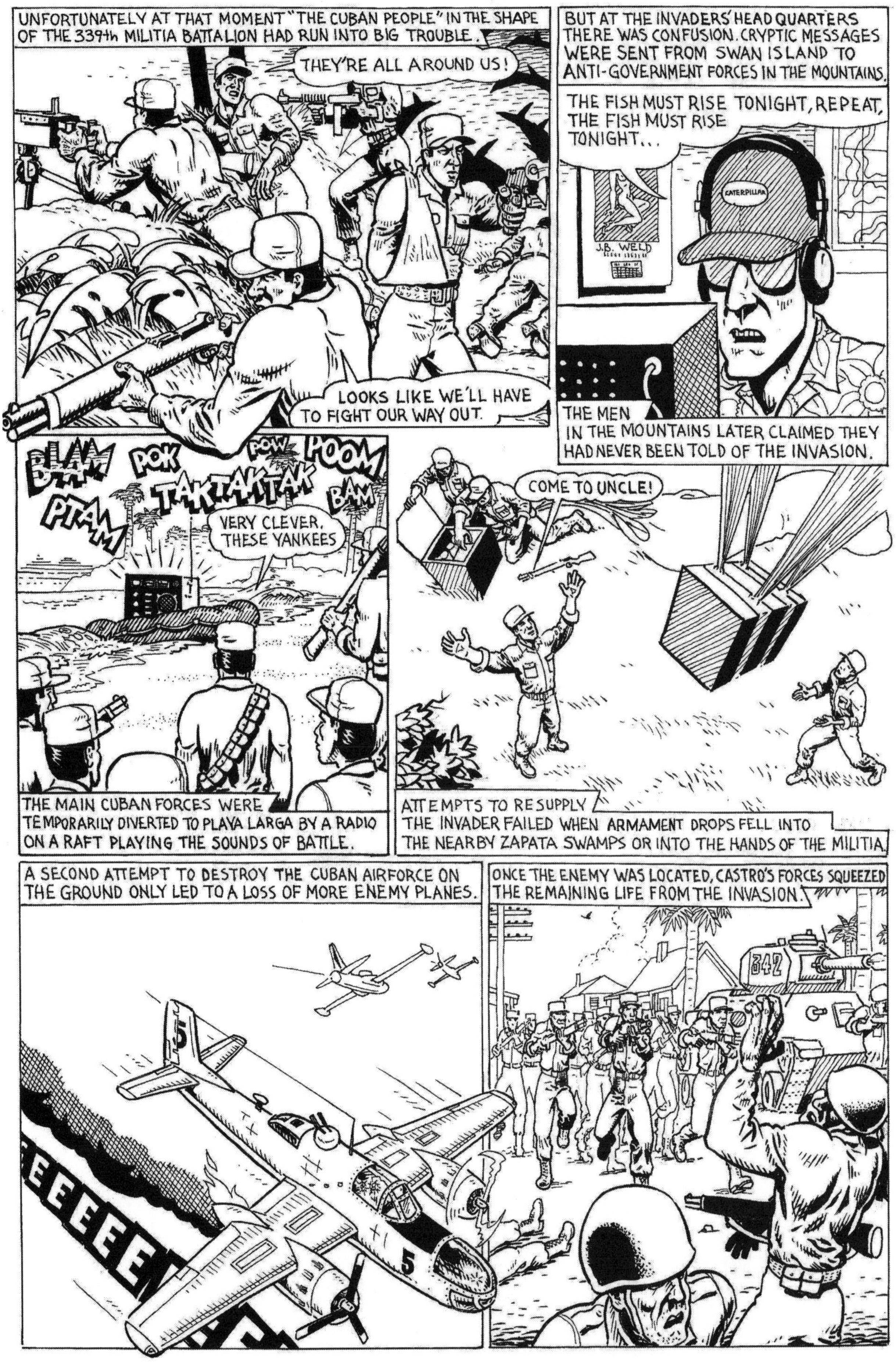
UNFORTUNATELY AT THAT MOMENT "THE CUBAN PEOPLE" IN THE SHAPE OF THE 339th MILITIA BATTALION HAD RUN INTO BIG TROUBLE.
THEY'RE ALL AROUND US!
LOOKS LIKE WE'LL HAVE TO FIGHT OUR WAY OUT.
BUT AT THE INVADERS' HEAD QUARTERS THERE WAS CONFUSION. CRYPTIC MESSAGES WERE SENT FROM SWAN ISLAND TO ANTI-GOVERNMENT FORCES IN THE MOUNTAINS.
THE FISH MUST RISE TONIGHT, REPEAT, THE FISH MUST RISE TONIGHT...
CATERPILLAR
J.B. WELD
THE MEN IN THE MOUNTAINS LATER CLAIMED THEY HAD NEVER BEEN TOLD OF THE INVASION.
BLAM POK POW POOM
PTAM TAKTAKTAK BAM
VERY CLEVER, THESE YANKEES
THE MAIN CUBAN FORCES WERE TEMPORARILY DIVERTED TO PLAYA LARGA BY A RADIO ON A RAFT PLAYING THE SOUNDS OF BATTLE.
COME TO UNCLE!
ATTEMPTS TO RESUPPLY THE INVADER FAILED WHEN ARMAMENT DROPS FELL INTO THE NEARBY ZAPATA SWAMPS OR INTO THE HANDS OF THE MILITIA.
A SECOND ATTEMPT TO DESTROY THE CUBAN AIRFORCE ON THE GROUND ONLY LED TO A LOSS OF MORE ENEMY PLANES.
EEEEEEE
ONCE THE ENEMY WAS LOCATED, CASTRO'S FORCES SQUEEZED THE REMAINING LIFE FROM THE INVASION.
342

WHEN THE BLAGAR AND THE ATLANTICO CAME TO RESCUE WHAT WAS LEFT OF THE INVADERS, FIGHTING BROKE OUT.

TWO U.S. DESTROYERS TURNED AWAY FROM THE CUBAN COAST WHEN THEY WERE FIRED UPON BY SHORE BATTERIES.

HAVING TRIED AND FAILED TO ENLIST LATIN AMERICAN SUPPORT TO OVERTHROW CASTRO, KENNEDY UNDERSTOOD THE DISASTROUS CONSEQUENCES OF OVERT AGGRESSION.

OVER 1000 COUNTER-REVOLUTIONARIES WHO DIDN'T MAKE IT TO THE RAFTS WERE TAKEN PRISONER.

I'M A COLONEL IN THE NATIONAL POLICE FORCE.

YOU'RE JUST ANOTHER BATISTA RAT TO US.

THE SECURITY SERVICE AND THE MILITIAS (THE ARMED PEOPLE OF CUBA) BOTH TRAINED BY CHE, HAD PERFORMED WELL.

CHE HIMSELF WAS HOSPITALIZED AFTER A GUN ACCIDENT AND WAS UNABLE TO PARTICIPATE DIRECTLY IN THE BATTLE.

OWW

BLAM

THE REVOLUTION HAD SURVIVED. CASTRO AND HIS TEAM'S PRESTIGE IN LATIN AMERICA GREW. CUBA HAD SHOWN IT WAS NOT ANOTHER GUATEMALA.

BY THE END OF 1961 MUCH OF THE CUBAN MILITARY AND THE ECONOMY WERE UNDER THE DIRECTION OF CHE.

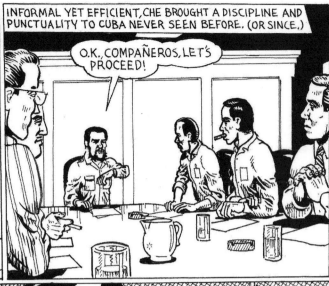

INFORMAL YET EFFICIENT, CHE BROUGHT A DISCIPLINE AND PUNCTUALITY TO CUBA NEVER SEEN BEFORE. (OR SINCE.)

O.K., COMPAÑEROS, LET'S PROCEED!

ONCE MEETINGS HAD BEGUN THE DOORS WERE LOCKED. EVEN GOVERNMENT MINISTERS WERE NOT ALLOWED IN.

BAM BAM BAM

ALTHOUGH HE HAD NO PREVIOUS EXPERIENCE IN BANKING, HE WAS ABLE TO FORGE AHEAD WITH THE GUIDANCE OF LATIN AMERICAN MARXIST ECONOMISTS.

CHE HAD FAR-REACHING PLANS FOR THE INDUSTRIALIZATION OF CUBA. WITH LARGE NICKEL DEPOSITS, TRUE ECONOMIC INDEPENDENCE SEEMED POSSIBLE.

U.S. PRESIDENT JOHN F. KENNEDY WAS ASTUTE ENOUGH TO UNDERSTAND THAT SOMETHING SIGNIFICANT WAS OCCURING IN LATIN AMERICA.

THOSE WHO MAKE REFORM IMPOSSIBLE MAKE REVOLUTION INEVITABLE.

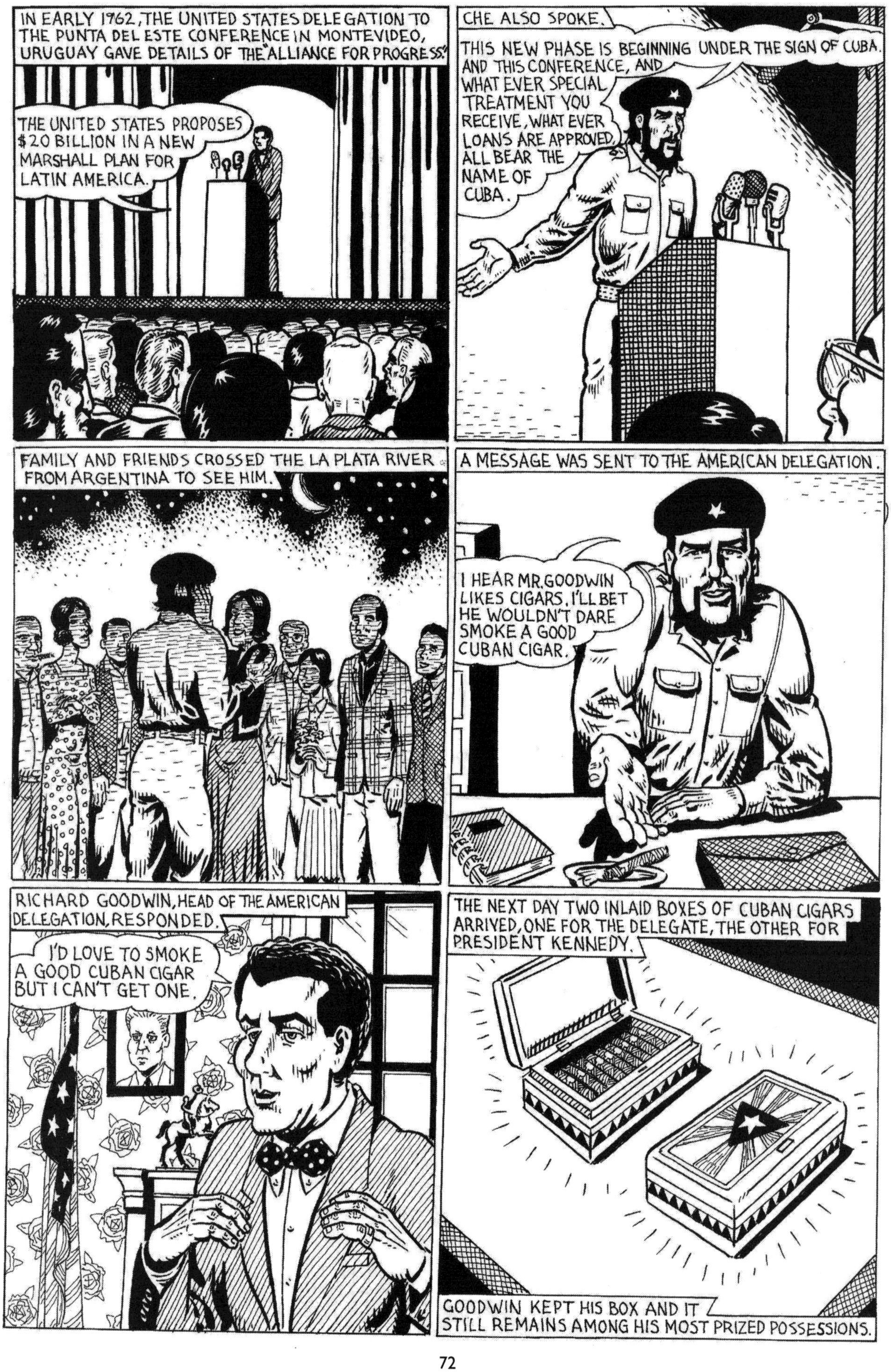

IN EARLY 1962, THE UNITED STATES DELEGATION TO THE PUNTA DEL ESTE CONFERENCE IN MONTEVIDEO, URUGUAY GAVE DETAILS OF THE "ALLIANCE FOR PROGRESS."
THE UNITED STATES PROPOSES $20 BILLION IN A NEW MARSHALL PLAN FOR LATIN AMERICA.
CHE ALSO SPOKE.
THIS NEW PHASE IS BEGINNING UNDER THE SIGN OF CUBA. AND THIS CONFERENCE, AND WHAT EVER SPECIAL TREATMENT YOU RECEIVE, WHAT EVER LOANS ARE APPROVED, ALL BEAR THE NAME OF CUBA.
FAMILY AND FRIENDS CROSSED THE LA PLATA RIVER FROM ARGENTINA TO SEE HIM.
A MESSAGE WAS SENT TO THE AMERICAN DELEGATION.
I HEAR MR. GOODWIN LIKES CIGARS. I'LL BET HE WOULDN'T DARE SMOKE A GOOD CUBAN CIGAR.
RICHARD GOODWIN, HEAD OF THE AMERICAN DELEGATION, RESPONDED.
I'D LOVE TO SMOKE A GOOD CUBAN CIGAR BUT I CAN'T GET ONE.
THE NEXT DAY TWO INLAID BOXES OF CUBAN CIGARS ARRIVED, ONE FOR THE DELEGATE, THE OTHER FOR PRESIDENT KENNEDY.
GOODWIN KEPT HIS BOX AND IT STILL REMAINS AMONG HIS MOST PRIZED POSSESSIONS.

KENNEDY DECIDED TO MAINTAIN SECRET CONTACTS WITH CUBA. ANY FORMAL RECOGNITION WOULD IMPLY ACCEPTANCE OF A COMMUNIST REGIME IN THE WESTERN HEMISPHERE.

IN CUBA ITSELF, THINGS WERE NOT GOING SO WELL. A DROUGHT AND DELIBERATE NEGLECT OF THE SUGAR CROP WERE TAKING A TOLL ON THE ECONOMY.

SOVIET BLOC AID FAILED TO LIVE UP TO EXPECTATIONS, CURTAILING HOPES FOR RAPID INDUSTRIALIZATION.

AS CHE'S AMBITIOUS PLANS BEGAN TO FALTER, INTENSE DISCUSSIONS WERE HELD WITH I.N.R.A. LEADER CARLOS RAFAEL RODRIGUEZ*

I STILL THINK WE NEED TO PRESS "MORAL INCENTIVES".

BUT, CHE, "MORAL INCENTIVES" ARE NOT REALLY MARXIST.

THE PEASANTS, WITH SMALL PLOTS OF THEIR OWN LAND, NO LONGER HAD TO RELY ON THE SEASONAL WORK OF CUTTING CANE.

BUT THE ATTEMPT TO SOLVE THIS PROBLEM, BY RECRUITING INEXPERIENCED URBAN WORKERS TO CUT CANE, PROVED UNECONOMICAL.

LAS VILLAS
1B37

* NO RELATION TO THE ARTIST

73

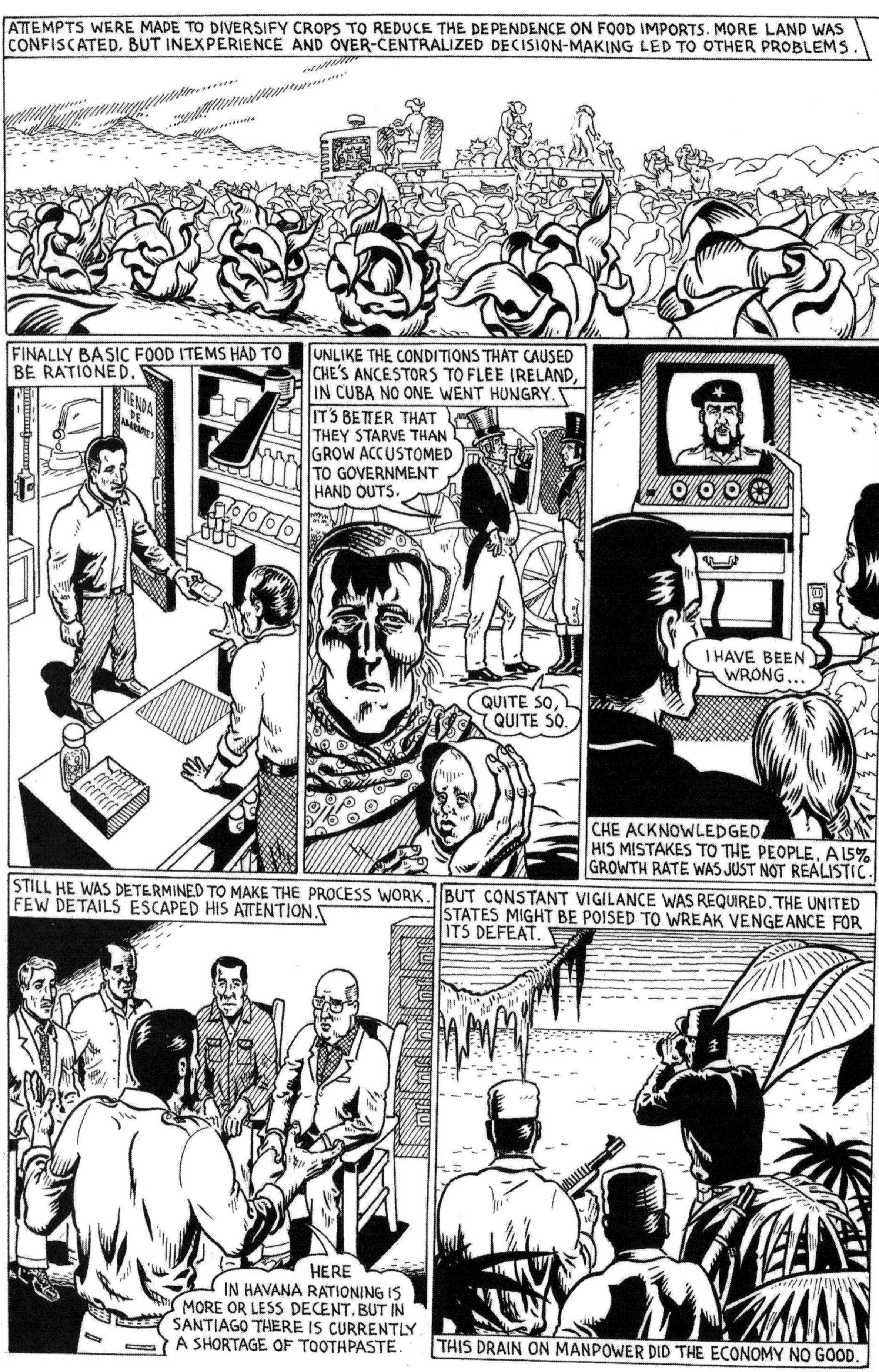
ATTEMPTS WERE MADE TO DIVERSIFY CROPS TO REDUCE THE DEPENDENCE ON FOOD IMPORTS. MORE LAND WAS CONFISCATED, BUT INEXPERIENCE AND OVER-CENTRALIZED DECISION-MAKING LED TO OTHER PROBLEMS.
FINALLY BASIC FOOD ITEMS HAD TO BE RATIONED.
TIENDA DE ABARROTES
UNLIKE THE CONDITIONS THAT CAUSED CHE'S ANCESTORS TO FLEE IRELAND, IN CUBA NO ONE WENT HUNGRY.
IT'S BETTER THAT THEY STARVE THAN GROW ACCUSTOMED TO GOVERNMENT HAND OUTS.
QUITE SO, QUITE SO.
I HAVE BEEN WRONG...
CHE ACKNOWLEDGED HIS MISTAKES TO THE PEOPLE. A 15% GROWTH RATE WAS JUST NOT REALISTIC.
STILL HE WAS DETERMINED TO MAKE THE PROCESS WORK. FEW DETAILS ESCAPED HIS ATTENTION.
HERE IN HAVANA RATIONING IS MORE OR LESS DECENT. BUT IN SANTIAGO THERE IS CURRENTLY A SHORTAGE OF TOOTHPASTE.
BUT CONSTANT VIGILANCE WAS REQUIRED. THE UNITED STATES MIGHT BE POISED TO WREAK VENGEANCE FOR ITS DEFEAT.
THIS DRAIN ON MANPOWER DID THE ECONOMY NO GOOD.

ON JANUARY 31, 1962 KENNEDY ASSURED ALEXEI ADZHUBEI, EDITOR OF IZVESTIA AND SON-IN-LAW TO SOVIET PREMIER KHRUSHCHEV...

I DO NOT FORESEE FOR THE TIME BEING ANY UNILATERAL ACTION AGAINST THE CASTRO REGIME.

BACK IN MOSCOW, ADZHUBEI REPORTED TO HIS FATHER-IN-LAW.

KENNEDY SAYS HE DOESN'T KNOW EXACTLY WHEN HE WILL ATTACK CUBA.

ENGLISH-RUSSIAN TRANSLATIONS ARE DIFFICULT. UNDER STRESS MISTAKES ARE OFTEN MADE.

CHE WAS SENT TO THE KREMLIN TO DISCUSS THE SITUATION.

AT FIRST CASTRO HAD MISGIVINGS ABOUT STATIONING MISSILES IN CUBA.

IF THE ISSUE IS ONLY OUR DEFENSE, THE DOWNSIDE IS HOW IT WILL AFFECT THE IMAGE OF THE REVOLUTION IN LATIN AMERICA. BUT IF IT WILL ALSO STRENGTHEN THE DEFENSE OF THE SOVIET BLOC, WE SHOULD ACCEPT.

SOON MYSTERIOUS TRUCKS WERE ROLLING THROUGH NEWLY WIDENED STREETS OF CUBAN TOWNS.

A U-2 SPY PLANE WAS SHOT DOWN OVER CUBA ON OCTOBER 27 BY A SOVIET ANTI-AIRCRAFT BATTERY.

75

BUT THE SURVEILLANCE PLANES KEPT COMING AND SOON THE SECRET WAS OUT.

MR. PRESIDENT, THESE PHOTOS ARE PROOF POSITIVE THAT THE RUSSIANS ARE BUILDING MISSILE BASES IN CUBA.

AT THE UNITED NATIONS, AMBASSADOR ADLAI STEVENSON PLAYED CAT-AND-MOUSE GAMES WITH THE SOVIETS OVER THE DEFINITION OF "OFFENSIVE WEAPONS."

THE SOVIET DELEGATE HAS FAILED TO RESPOND TO MY QUESTION AS TO WHETHER THERE ARE OFFENSIVE WEAPONS IN CUBA.

THE UNITED STATES OF AMERICA

I AM STILL AWAITING AN ANSWER.

THEY DIDN'T REALISE THAT, OF THE 42 MISSILES THAT THE SOVIETS HAD INSTALLED, TWENTY WERE ALREADY EQUIPPED WITH NUCLEAR WARHEADS AND READY TO GO.

BLOCKADE IS SUCH AN UGLY WORD. IT WILL REMIND PEOPLE OF THE BERLIN BLOCKADE OF '49.

KENNEDY DECIDED TO IMPOSE A "QUARANTINE" AROUND CUBA.

THE U.S. NAVY WAS AUTHORIZED TO STOP AND BOARD SOVIET SHIPS ON THE HIGH SEAS HEADED FOR CUBA, AN ACT OF WAR AGAINST THE OTHER MAJOR NUCLEAR POWER.

85

ON A PERSONAL NOTE, I REMEMBER THIS TIME CLEARLY. I WAS ON A BUS AND OF COURSE I WAS AWARE THAT EVERYTHING MIGHT ABRUPTLY GO UP IN A FLASH. I REMEMBER LOOKING AT THE OTHER RIDERS. ON EACH PERSON'S FACE I COULD CLEARLY SEE A LOOK OF FEAR AND DREAD.

WE'RE ON THE BRINK OF W.W. III ALL THIS COULD END ANY SECOND.

AM I THE ONLY ONE WHO IS THINKING ABOUT THIS?

EVERYONE IS SCARED OUT OF THEIR WITS!

AND THE WORLD HELD ITS BREATH AS SOVIET SHIPS EDGED CLOSER TO THE U.S. NAVY'S "QUARANTINE".

WHAT FEW OF US UNDERSTOOD IS THAT AN H-BOMB USES AN A-BOMB AS ITS TRIGGER.

YES, BUT IF WE INVADE CUBA DON'T WE THEN HAVE TO WORRY ABOUT THE SOVIETS INVADING BERLIN, WHERE WE ARE IN A FAR LESS ADVANTAGEOUS STRATEGIC POSITION?

KENNEDY RESISTED CALLS TO ESCALATE.

THE KNOWLEDGE THAT, BESIDES AN ARMED POPULACE, 40,000 SOVIET TROOPS AND TACTICAL NUCLEAR WEAPONS AWAITED HIM ON THE ISLAND MIGHT HAVE FURTHER GIVEN HIM PAUSE.

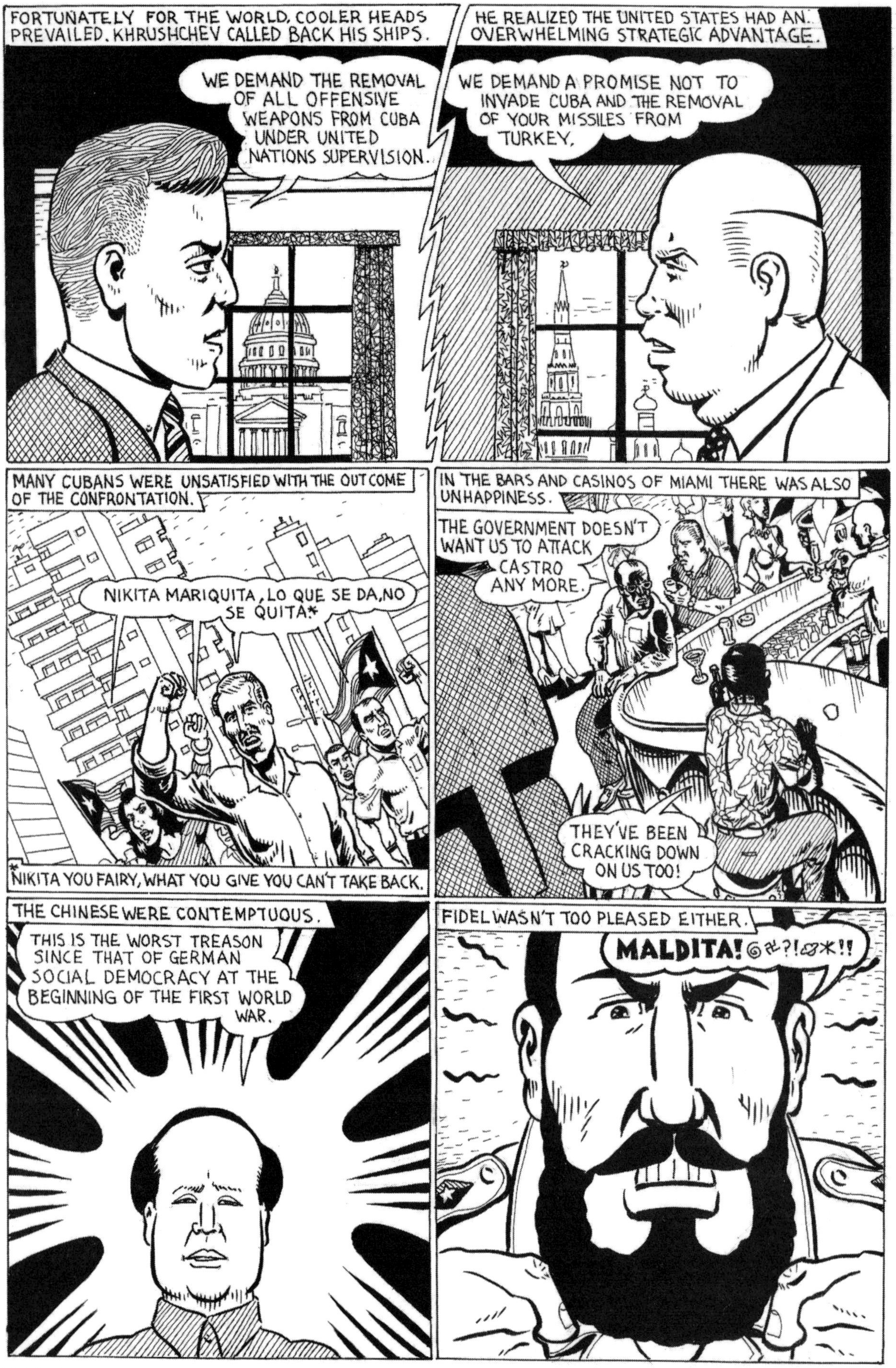
FORTUNATELY FOR THE WORLD, COOLER HEADS PREVAILED. KHRUSHCHEV CALLED BACK HIS SHIPS.
WE DEMAND THE REMOVAL OF ALL OFFENSIVE WEAPONS FROM CUBA UNDER UNITED NATIONS SUPERVISION.
HE REALIZED THE UNITED STATES HAD AN OVERWHELMING STRATEGIC ADVANTAGE.
WE DEMAND A PROMISE NOT TO INVADE CUBA AND THE REMOVAL OF YOUR MISSILES FROM TURKEY.
MANY CUBANS WERE UNSATISFIED WITH THE OUTCOME OF THE CONFRONTATION.
NIKITA MARIQUITA, LO QUE SE DA, NO SE QUITA.*
*NIKITA YOU FAIRY, WHAT YOU GIVE YOU CAN'T TAKE BACK.
IN THE BARS AND CASINOS OF MIAMI THERE WAS ALSO UNHAPPINESS.
THE GOVERNMENT DOESN'T WANT US TO ATTACK CASTRO ANY MORE.
THEY'VE BEEN CRACKING DOWN ON US TOO!
THE CHINESE WERE CONTEMPTUOUS.
THIS IS THE WORST TREASON SINCE THAT OF GERMAN SOCIAL DEMOCRACY AT THE BEGINNING OF THE FIRST WORLD WAR.
FIDEL WASN'T TOO PLEASED EITHER.
MALDITA!

DURING THE CRISIS CHE'S COMMAND WAS GIVEN THE TASK OF REPULSING ANY ATTACK ON THE WESTERN REGION.

CHE, HIMSELF, HAD BEEN WILLING TO GO DOWN IN A BLAZE OF NUCLEAR GLORY.

YOU HAVE THE HARROWING EXAMPLE OF A PEOPLE READY TO SACRIFICE ITSELF TO NUCLEAR ARMS, THAT ITS ASHES MIGHT SERVE AS A BASIS FOR NEW SOCIETIES. AND WHEN AN AGREEMENT IS REACHED WITHOUT EVEN CONSULTING IT, AND ATOMIC MISSILES ARE WITHDRAWN, IT DOES NOT BREATHE A SIGH OF RELIEF. IT ENTERS THE FRAY TO MAKE KNOWN ITS OWN UNIQUE VOICE.

HIS SOVIET FRIEND, ANASTAS MIKOYAN, TRIED TO EXPLAIN THE SOVIET VIEW POINT.

WE DID EVERYTHING WE COULD SO THAT CUBA WOULD NOT BE DESTROYED. WE SEE YOUR READINESS TO DIE BEAUTIFULLY, BUT WE BELIEVE IT ISN'T WORTH DYING BEAUTIFULLY.

CUBA'S DEMANDS WERE IGNORED. THE U.S. STILL OCCUPIED THE BASE AT GUANTÁNAMO.

CUBANS COULD ONLY WATCH IMPOTENTLY AS U-2 AIRCRAFT VIOLATED CUBA'S AIRSPACE.

KHRUSHCHEV SENT CASTRO A LETTER ACKNOWLEDGING THE STRAIN IN CUBAN-SOVIET RELATIONS AND INVITING HIM TO RUSSIA TO GO HUNTING.

MOST HONORED COMRADE FIDEL IT SEEMS TO ME THAT THIS CRISIS HAS LEFT A MARK, ALTHOUGH BARELY VISIBLE, IN THE RELATIONS BETWEEN OUR STATES. SPEAKING FRANKLY, RELATIONS ARE NOT WHAT THEY WERE BEFORE THE CRISIS. DURING THE CARIBBEAN CRISIS OUR VIEWPOINTS DIDN'T ALWAYS COINCIDE. WE DID NOT SEE THE DIFFERENT STAGES OF THE CRISIS IN THE SAME WAY. I WILL NOT HIDE FROM YOU, IT WOULD BE SENSELESS TO DO SO, THAT ANY IMPRUDENT STEP OR EVEN ANY ROUGHNESS IN OUR RELATIONS COULD GENERATE SEVERAL PROBLEMS. ONE ILL-ADVISED STEP OR ONE WRONG SENTENCE COULD MAKE US AND YOU T...

CASTRO ACCEPTED KHRUSHCHEV'S INVITATION AND NEW TRADE AGREEMENTS WERE SIGNED.

79

CHE'S FIRST SON, BORN IN 1962, WAS NAMED AFTER CAMILO CIENFUEGOS.

IN 1963 HIS DAUGHTER CELIA WAS BORN.

BY 1966 HIS FAMILY HAD GROWN TO SIX.

DURING A TRIP TO INDIA, A HOTEL WORKER SNUCK A PEEK AT CHE'S PASSIONATE CORRESPONDENCE WITH ALEIDA. HE WAS SHOCKED.

PORNOGRAPHY!

HIS MODEST HOUSEHOLD WAS RUN WITH THE SAME SPARTAN REVOLUTIONARY ETHIC AS HIS WORKPLACE.

NO, ALEIDA, THAT CAR BELONGS TO THE CUBAN PEOPLE. IT'S ONLY FOR OFFICIAL BUSINESS.

BUT WHEN CHE WASN'T AROUND, ALEIDA TOOK THE OFFICIAL CAR.

IF I HAD TAKEN THE BUS AND THEN HAD TO WAIT IN LINE IT WOULD'VE BEEN HOURS.

I THINK THIS SHIFT IN ASSIGNMENTS WILL HELP COMRADE CHE TO BETTER FOCUS HIS ATTENTION ON MORE PRESSING MATTERS.

AS TIME PASSED, SOME OF HIS RESPONSIBILITIES BEGAN TO BE TAKEN UP BY OTHERS.

SINCE THE MISSILE CRISIS CHE'S LINE HAD HARDENED. HE NO LONGER THOUGHT REVOLUTION WAS IMPOSSIBLE IN CONSTITUTIONAL DEMOCRACIES.

I BELIEVE THAT REVOLUTION CAN BE CREATED IN ANY COUNTRY BY A DETERMINED VANGUARD.

WE MUST FIGHT THIS DISEASE OF COMMUNISM IN OUR HEMISPHERE.

BUT CUBA'S SUPPORT FOR INSURGENCIES IN LATIN AMERICA LED TO ITS DENUNCIATION AND EXPULSION FROM THE ORGANIZATION OF AMERICAN STATES (O.A.S.).

CHE ASSEMBLED REPRESENTATIVES FROM ALL ARGENTINE ANTI-GOVERNMENT FACTIONS FROM PERONISTS TO TROTSKYISTS.

IT SOON BECAME APPARENT THAT THE PROSPECT OF ARMED INSURRECTION WITH THIS SQUABBLING GROUP WAS DIM.

WE REGARD STALINISTS AS JUST ANOTHER MILITARY CLIQUE.

THE HOPED-FOR UPRISINGS FAILED TO FIND SUCCESS.

A SIGNIFICANT FACTOR IN THIS FAILURE WAS THE LACK OF SUPPORT FROM LOCAL COMMUNIST PARTIES.

THE MASSES WILL MAKE REVOLUTION WHEN THEY ARE READY. ANYTHING ELSE IS PREMATURE ADVENTURISM.

FIDEL, EVER THE PRACTICAL POLITICIAN, HAD MADE HIS PEACE WITH KHRUSHCHEV.

THE SOVIETS, FOR THEIR PART, PAID LIP SERVICE TO CASTRO'S IDEAS EVEN THOUGH THEY THOUGHT THE TIME FOR REVOLUTION IN LATIN AMERICA HAD PASSED.

AFRICA WAS A DIFFERENT STORY. IN MID-1963 CHE VISITED HIS OLD FRIEND AND FIRST PRESIDENT OF INDEPENDENT ALGERIA, BEN BELLA.

AFTER A MOROCCAN BORDER ATTACK, CUBA SENT ALGERIA 700 MEN AND 22 TANKS. KING HASSAN SOON OPENED NEGOTIATIONS.

CHE SAW THE POTENTIAL FOR UPHEAVAL IN AFRICA, A CONCLUSION AT WHICH THE CIA HAD ALREADY ARRIVED.

ACCORDING TO OUR LATEST REPORTS THERE ARE NUMEROUS AREAS IN AFRICA ABOUT TO GO OFF THE RESERVATION.

INDEED, THE BRUTAL MURDER OF PATRICE LUMUMBA, THE NEWLY-LIBERATED CONGO'S FIRST PRESIDENT, HAD LEFT A BITTER TASTE IN THE MOUTHS OF MANY.

AT THE OPENING OF THE INTERNATIONAL AFRICAN ASSOCIATION IN 1876 KING LEOPOLD II OF BELGIUM PROCLAIMED ITS PURPOSE.

...TO OPEN TO CIVILIZATION THE ONLY PART OF OUR GLOBE WHICH IT HAS NOT PENETRATED, TO PIERCE THE DARKNESS WHICH HANGS OVER ENTIRE PEOPLES.

HE THEN INITIATED A CAMPAIGN OF SAVAGE ATROCITIES TO COERCE NATIVE PEOPLE INTO LABOR EVEN THOUGH SLAVERY WAS OFFICIALLY ABOLISHED.

WHEN THE PEOPLE OF THE CONGO FINALLY ROSE UP IN 1960 AFTER DECADES OF TORMENT AND EXPLOITATION, THE RESULTS WERE NOT PRETTY.

AFTER MURDERING PRESIDENT LUMUMBA, WESTERN POWERS MANAGED TO INSTALL A KLEPTOCRACY UNDER PREENING JOSEPH MOBUTO.

THE CHAOTIC SITUATION HAD BEEN THE IDEAL PRETEXT, SEIZED ON BY OTHER IMPERIALIST NATIONS SUCH AS THE U.S. AND FRANCE.

MEANWHILE, CHE SPOKE TO THE SOVIET AMBASSADOR BEFORE A VISIT TO MOSCOW WITH CASTRO.

I FEAR I'M SEEN AS A TROUBLE MAKER AND AN UGLY DUCKLING IN YOUR COUNTRY.

I KNOW THE OPPOSITE IS TRUE, BECAUSE IN MY COUNTRY YOU ARE APPRECIATED PRECISELY FOR YOUR FIRMNESS IN DEFENDING YOUR IDEAS EVEN THOUGH THEY ARE SOMETIMES WRONG, AND FOR YOUR COURAGE IN RECONIZING YOUR MISTAKES, AND A CERTAIN TASTE FOR TROUBLEMAKING IS NOT A DEFICIT IN OUR EYES.

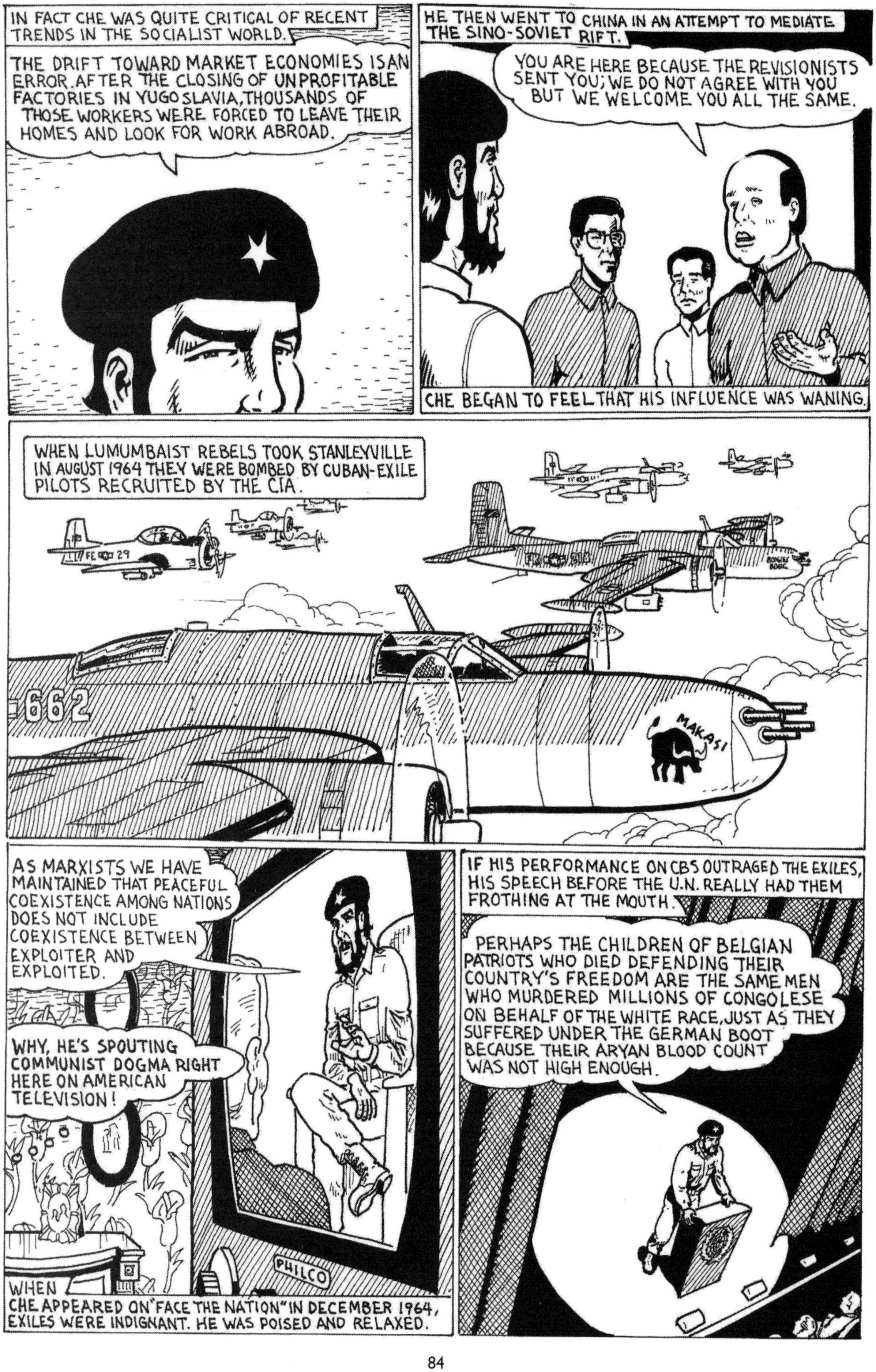

IN FACT CHE WAS QUITE CRITICAL OF RECENT TRENDS IN THE SOCIALIST WORLD.
THE DRIFT TOWARD MARKET ECONOMIES IS AN ERROR. AFTER THE CLOSING OF UNPROFITABLE FACTORIES IN YUGOSLAVIA, THOUSANDS OF THOSE WORKERS WERE FORCED TO LEAVE THEIR HOMES AND LOOK FOR WORK ABROAD.
HE THEN WENT TO CHINA IN AN ATTEMPT TO MEDIATE THE SINO-SOVIET RIFT.
YOU ARE HERE BECAUSE THE REVISIONISTS SENT YOU; WE DO NOT AGREE WITH YOU BUT WE WELCOME YOU ALL THE SAME.
CHE BEGAN TO FEEL THAT HIS INFLUENCE WAS WANING.
WHEN LUMUMBAIST REBELS TOOK STANLEYVILLE IN AUGUST 1964 THEY WERE BOMBED BY CUBAN-EXILE PILOTS RECRUITED BY THE CIA.
FE 29
662
MAKASI
AS MARXISTS WE HAVE MAINTAINED THAT PEACEFUL COEXISTENCE AMONG NATIONS DOES NOT INCLUDE COEXISTENCE BETWEEN EXPLOITER AND EXPLOITED.
WHY, HE'S SPOUTING COMMUNIST DOGMA RIGHT HERE ON AMERICAN TELEVISION!
PHILCO
WHEN CHE APPEARED ON "FACE THE NATION" IN DECEMBER 1964, EXILES WERE INDIGNANT. HE WAS POISED AND RELAXED.
IF HIS PERFORMANCE ON CBS OUTRAGED THE EXILES, HIS SPEECH BEFORE THE U.N. REALLY HAD THEM FROTHING AT THE MOUTH.
PERHAPS THE CHILDREN OF BELGIAN PATRIOTS WHO DIED DEFENDING THEIR COUNTRY'S FREEDOM ARE THE SAME MEN WHO MURDERED MILLIONS OF CONGOLESE ON BEHALF OF THE WHITE RACE, JUST AS THEY SUFFERED UNDER THE GERMAN BOOT BECAUSE THEIR ARYAN BLOOD COUNT WAS NOT HIGH ENOUGH.

THE EVENT CHE WAS REFERRING TO WAS THE MASSACRE OF CIVILIANS BY BELGIAN AND OTHER EUROPEAN TROOPS DURING THE RETAKING OF STANLEYVILLE.

ALTHOUGH ATROCITIES WERE COMMITTED BY BOTH SIDES, THE MOST GRISLY EVENT WAS THE DISMEMBERMENT OF SURRENDERED REBEL LEADER PIERRE MULELE, IN 1968. ON ORDERS FROM MOBUTO, HIS TORSO WAS FED TO THE CROCODILES.

IN GUINEA GUEVARA CALLED FOR UNITY AMONG ANTI-COLONIALIST MOVEMENTS AND CLOSER, BUT NOT TOO CLOSE, TIES WITH THE SOVIET UNION AND CHINA.

IT'S CRUCIAL NOT TO ALLOW ANY OTHER NATION TO HAVE TOO MUCH INFLUENCE ON YOUR ECONOMY.

HE MET AGOSTINHO NETO, THE FUTURE PRESIDENT OF POST-COLONIAL ANGOLA. THIS FIRST CONTACT WOULD HAVE PROFOUND CONSEQUENCES FOR AFRICA.

YAWN

MY NAME IS GODEFROI CHAMALESO. WELCOME!

ERNESTO CHE GUEVARA HAD ARRIVED IN THE CONGO.

HE WAS BACK IN HIS ELEMENT.

WE ARE HAVING A SMALL MEETING AT BASE COMMAND WOULD YOU LIKE TO ATTEND?

YES.

MANY OF THESE MEN APPEAR TO BE BE SHOWING GODEFROI VERY LITTLE RESPECT.

HE FOUND THAT MEN FROM THE FRONT LINES BORE A RESENTMENT OF THOSE WHO WORKED IN THE REAR.

GODEFROI HAD INCURRED A GREAT DEAL OF DISLIKE BECAUSE HIS DUTIES CAUSED HIM TO SPEND MUCH TIME IN DAR-ES-SALAAM ON THE EAST COAST OF AFRICA.

CHE BECAME ACQUAINTED WITH SOME OF THE FIGHTERS.

WE DO NOT FEAR ENEMY AIRCRAFT BECAUSE OF OUR SECRET WEAPON, THE DAWA MEDICINE WHICH MAKES US INVULNERABLE TO GUNFIRE.

I ADMIRE YOUR COURAGE. YOU LAUGH IN THE FACE OF THE ENEMY'S FIRE POWER.

IT IS NOT A JOKE, MY FRIEND.

I MYSELF HAVE BEEN SHOT. I SAW THE BULLETS BOUNCE OFF MY CHEST AND FALL HARMLESSLY ON THE GROUND.

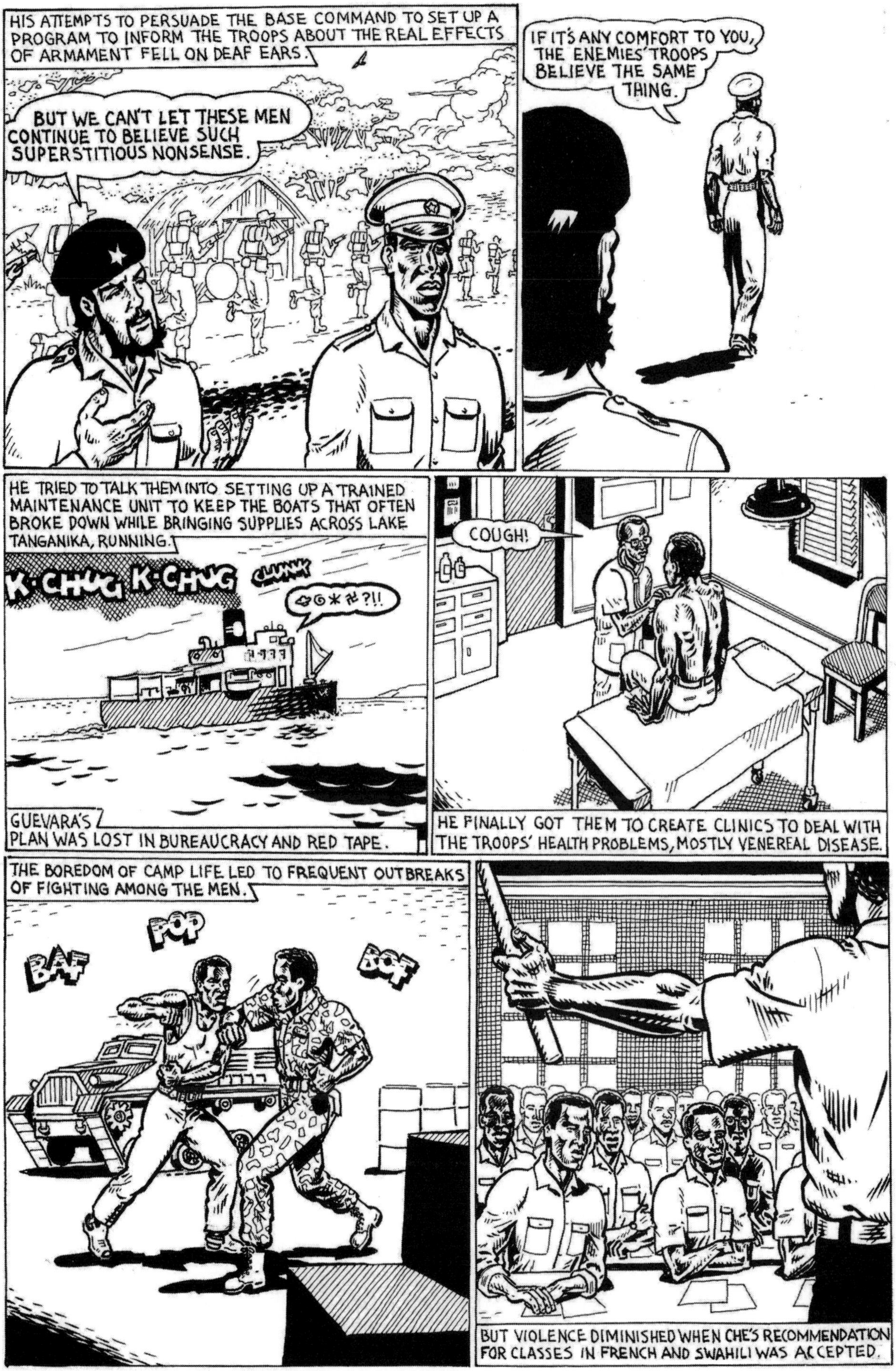

HIS ATTEMPTS TO PERSUADE THE BASE COMMAND TO SET UP A PROGRAM TO INFORM THE TROOPS ABOUT THE REAL EFFECTS OF ARMAMENT FELL ON DEAF EARS.
BUT WE CAN'T LET THESE MEN CONTINUE TO BELIEVE SUCH SUPERSTITIOUS NONSENSE.
IF IT'S ANY COMFORT TO YOU, THE ENEMIES' TROOPS BELIEVE THE SAME THING.
HE TRIED TO TALK THEM INTO SETTING UP A TRAINED MAINTENANCE UNIT TO KEEP THE BOATS THAT OFTEN BROKE DOWN WHILE BRINGING SUPPLIES ACROSS LAKE TANGANIKA, RUNNING.
K-CHUG K-CHUG
CLUNK
?!!
GUEVARA'S PLAN WAS LOST IN BUREAUCRACY AND RED TAPE.
COUGH!
HE FINALLY GOT THEM TO CREATE CLINICS TO DEAL WITH THE TROOPS' HEALTH PROBLEMS, MOSTLY VENEREAL DISEASE.
THE BOREDOM OF CAMP LIFE LED TO FREQUENT OUTBREAKS OF FIGHTING AMONG THE MEN.
BAF
POP
BOF
BUT VIOLENCE DIMINISHED WHEN CHE'S RECOMMENDATION FOR CLASSES IN FRENCH AND SWAHILI WAS ACCEPTED.

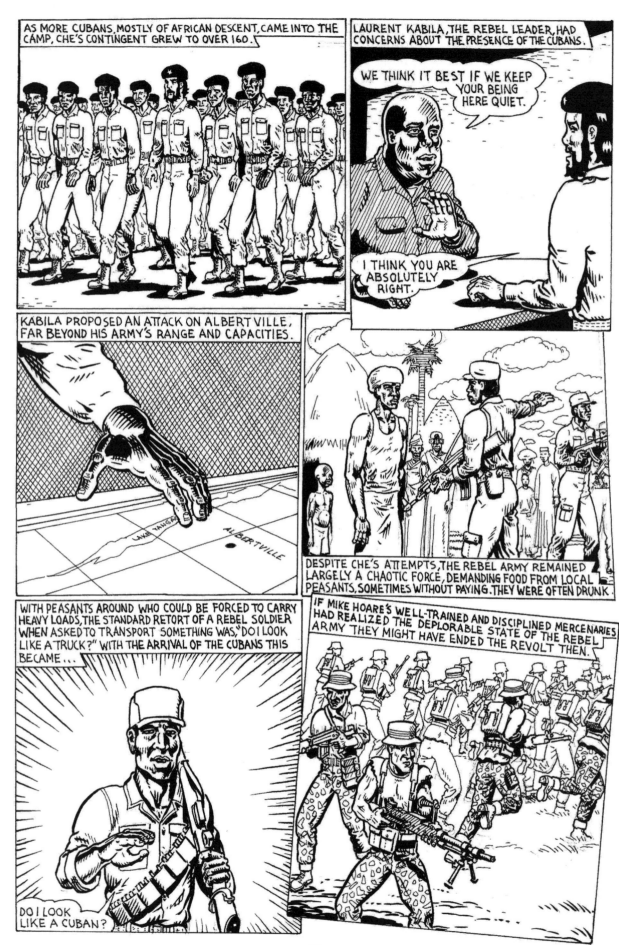

AS MORE CUBANS, MOSTLY OF AFRICAN DESCENT, CAME INTO THE CAMP, CHE'S CONTINGENT GREW TO OVER 160.

LAURENT KABILA, THE REBEL LEADER, HAD CONCERNS ABOUT THE PRESENCE OF THE CUBANS.

WE THINK IT BEST IF WE KEEP YOUR BEING HERE QUIET.

I THINK YOU ARE ABSOLUTELY RIGHT.

KABILA PROPOSED AN ATTACK ON ALBERTVILLE, FAR BEYOND HIS ARMY'S RANGE AND CAPACITIES.

LAKE TANGA.

ALBERTVILLE

DESPITE CHE'S ATTEMPTS, THE REBEL ARMY REMAINED LARGELY A CHAOTIC FORCE, DEMANDING FOOD FROM LOCAL PEASANTS, SOMETIMES WITHOUT PAYING. THEY WERE OFTEN DRUNK.

WITH PEASANTS AROUND WHO COULD BE FORCED TO CARRY HEAVY LOADS, THE STANDARD RETORT OF A REBEL SOLDIER WHEN ASKED TO TRANSPORT SOMETHING WAS, "DO I LOOK LIKE A TRUCK?" WITH THE ARRIVAL OF THE CUBANS THIS BECAME...

DO I LOOK LIKE A CUBAN?

IF MIKE HOARE'S WELL-TRAINED AND DISCIPLINED MERCENARIES HAD REALIZED THE DEPLORABLE STATE OF THE REBEL ARMY THEY MIGHT HAVE ENDED THE REVOLT THEN.

88

THE HEAT AND STRESS TOOK ITS TOLL ON CHE, BRINGING ON A NEW BOUT OF ASTHMA.

KHAF KHAF

BRAAAPHT

THE CUBANS CONVINCED KABILA THAT AN AMBUSH AT LA FORCE, A CLOSER TARGET, WAS MORE PRACTICAL. THE ADRENALINE OF THE FORTHCOMING BATTLE RELIEVED CHE'S ASTHMA.

...AND REMEMBER, PUT YOUR TROOPS ON ONLY ONE SIDE OF THE ROAD TO AVOID SHOOTING YOUR OWN MEN.

SQUABBLING SOON BROKE OUT WHEN IT WAS LEARNED THAT SOME VILLAGERS HAD REPORTED THEM. SOME WANTED TO TURN BACK.

LET'S PUT IT TO A VOTE.

AFTER THE VOTE THE MISSION WAS ABORTED.

A RECONNAISSANCE PATROL CAPTURED THREE POLICEMEN WHO WERE CUTTING GRASS ON THE SIDE OF THE ROAD TO IMPROVE VISIBILITY. ONE TRIED TO ESCAPE AND WAS SHOT.

WHEN THE MEN REPORTED BACK CHE HAD SOMETHING TO SAY TO THEM.

REVOLUTIONARY DEMOCRACY HAS NEVER BEEN APPLIED IN RUNNING ARMIES ANYWHERE IN THE WORLD AND ANY ATTEMPT TO IMPLEMENT IT HAS ENDED IN DISASTER.

THE BEWILDERING NUMBER OF TRIBAL ALLEGIANCES MADE FORGING A NATIONAL IDENTITY A DAUNTING TASK, BUT CHE DID HIS BEST TO TRAIN AND INSTILL A SENSE OF PURPOSE IN THE CONGOLESE REBELS.

CHE FINALLY GOT PERMISSION TO VISIT THE FRONT. THIS DID NOT REFLECT WELL ON KABILA, WHO WOULD NEVER LEAVE DAR-ES-SALAAM.

LATER, A SUCCESSFUL AMBUSH OF A TRUCK CONVOY WAS CARRIED OUT BY A JOINT FORCE OF CUBANS AND REBELS.

FRAM

WHEN BOOZE WAS FOUND IN THE TRUCKS THE AFRICANS PROCEEDED TO GET DRUNK, AS THE CUBANS LOOKED ON.

THE ATTACK ON LA FORCE WAS NOT SUCCESSFUL AND WORSE, A DEAD CUBAN SOLDIER WAS IDENTIFIED BY PAPERS HE HAD BEEN CARRYING AGAINST THE EXPLICIT ORDERS OF CHE.

WHAT DO WE HAVE HERE?

THE ONLY THING THAT SAVED THE REBEL ARMY WAS THAT THE CONGOLESE ARMY WAS WORSE, OFTEN FLEEING AFTER THE FIRST SHOT. THEIR EXAGGERATED ACCOUNTS OF THE REBELS WERE BELIEVED BY THEIR AMERICAN AND SOUTH AFRICAN HANDLERS.

BLAM
POUM
POP
BDAM
BAM

AS CUBAN MORALE BEGAN TO PLUMMET, CHE BECAME MORE IRASCIBLE.

COMANDANTE, THE SHIPMENT OF VITAMINS FOR THE TROOPS HAS ARRIVED.

VITAMINS? THE CONGOLESE DON'T HAVE VITAMINS. WHY SHOULD WE?

IN NOVEMBER 1965 A DISCOURAGED AND EXHAUSTED CHE LEFT THE CONGO. HIS CUBAN CONTINGENT WAS HAPPY TO GO. THEY HAD DONE THEIR BEST TO GIVE SOME COHERENCE TO A CHAOTIC SITUATION.

THE CUBANS SLIPPED OUT OF THE COUNTRY IN GOOD ORDER, ANGERING THE EXILED "GUSANOS"* FIGHTING THERE.

I DIDN'T GET TO KILL EVEN ONE FIDELISTA.

* SPANISH FOR WORM, THE CUBAN TERM FOR ANTI-CASTRO EXILES

LAURENT KABILA DROVE OUT MOBUTO IN 1997, NO DOUBT HAVING ABSORBED SOME OF THE LESSONS CHE HAD ATTEMPTED TO IMPART.

IN JANUARY OF 2001 HE WAS ASSASSINATED.

BACK IN CUBA CHE SPENT TIME REREADING LENIN AND STALIN, MAKING NOTES ON HIS OBSERVATIONS AND CRITICISMS.

THESE PEOPLE NEED TO BE DE-LOUSED BEFORE THEY'RE ALLOWED TO ENTER MY OFFICE.

YEARS BEFORE, WHILE TRAVELING THROUGH BOLIVIA, HE HAD WITNESSED THE HUMILIATION OF A GROUP OF NATIVE PEOPLE TRYING TO MEET WITH A GOVERNMENT OFFICIAL. IT MADE A LASTING IMPRESSION ON THE YOUNG ERNESTO.

91

NOW CHE SET HIS SIGHTS ON THAT COUNTRY. HE WAS ABOUT TO SET OUT ON HIS LAST ADVENTURE.

HE BEGAN THE PAINFUL PROCESS OF CHANGING HIS APPEARANCE IN ORDER TO MAKE HIS WAY INTO BOLIVIA UNDETECTED.

HE WAS TRANSFORMED INTO A TRAVELING BUSINESSMAN NAMED RAMON.

SNIP SNIP SNIP

OW!

PLUCK

DO YOU WANT ME TO SLOW DOWN?

NO, NO, JUST KEEP ON AS YOU'VE BEEN DOING.

AT A FAREWELL DINNER FOR CHE AND HIS EXPEDITION IN OCTOBER 1966, CASTRO REMINISCED ABOUT THEIR DAYS IN THE SIERRA MAESTRA.

CHE LEFT AND THE PARTY WOUND DOWN. FIDEL WAS SEEN WALKING OUT OF THE ROOM. HE SUSPECTED THIS WAS THE LAST TIME HE WOULD SEE HIS OLD COMRADE ALIVE.

CHE SAID GOODBYE TO HIS CHILDREN DISGUISED AS UNCLE RAMON. HE PROMISED TO PASS A KISS ALONG TO THEIR FATHER. THEY WERE TOO YOUNG TO KEEP A SECRET.

HE HAD A SPECIAL MEETING WITH HIS YOUNGEST DAUGHTER. AFTERWARD, SHE RAN BACK TO HER MOTHER. HE COULD HEAR HER SAY...

MOMMY, I THINK THAT MAN RAMON IS IN LOVE WITH ME.

AS HE TOLD ALEIDA, SHE WOULD HAVE NO MEMORY OF THIS.

THE MAIN IMPEDIMENT TO REVOLUTION IN LATIN AMERICA WAS THE RELUCTANCE OF LOCAL COMMUNIST PARTIES.

NO! OUR COUNTRY IS NOT READY FOR GUERRILLA WAR!

BUT THE YOUTH WING OF THE BOLIVIAN COMMUNIST PARTY WAS ENTHUSIASTICALLY PRO-CASTRO.

BAJO CON IMPERIALISMO

CON FIDEL

VIVA CASTRO

THE ARID HIGHLANDS OF ÑANCAHUAZU IN SOUTH EASTERN BOLIVIA WAS A POOR CHOICE FOR GUERRILLA WARFARE. CASTRO KNEW THAT A DETERMINED CHE COULD NOT BE DISSUADED FROM HIS COURSE AND TRIED TO STEER HIM TO THE JUNGLES IN THE NORTH WESTERN PART OF THE COUNTRY. THE LEADERSHIP OF THE BOLIVIAN C.P., HOWEVER, WANTED TO PLACE HIM NOT TOO FAR FROM THE ARGENTINE BORDER, IN HOPES THAT CIRCUMSTANCES WOULD SOON PUSH HIM OUT OF THE COUNTRY.

THE CHOICE OF ÑANCAHUAZU WAS THE RESULT OF MUCH DUPLICITY AND CONFUSION AMONG ALL PARTIES INVOLVED. CHE, HIMSELF, HAD NEVER ABANDONED HIS DREAMS OF FOMENTING REVOLUTION IN HIS NATIVE ARGENTINA, SO HE AND HIS MEN TREKKED ACROSS THIS BARREN AND INHOSPITABLE LAND TOWARD THEIR BASE.

WHEN THE MEN, EXHAUSTED AND FAMISHED, REACHED THEIR DESTINATION THEY GORGED ON THE ROASTED LAMB THAT HAD BEEN PREPARED FOR THEM.

30. CAL

30. CAL

ALL CLANDESTINE LOGISTICAL OPERATIONS HAD BEEN EFFICIENTLY HANDLED BY A CUBAN AGENT CODE-NAMED TANIA.

ATTEMPTS TO FOMENT REVOLUTION IN ARGENTINA HAD BEEN TRIED BEFORE, WITH DISASTROUS RESULTS. ARGENTINA'S POLICE FORCE WAS BRUTAL AND EFFECTIVE.

THE PRESIDENT OF BOLIVIA, RENÉ BARRIENTOS, ENJOYED THE UNQUALIFIED SUPPORT OF THE UNITED STATES. BESIDES LARGE AMOUNTS OF AID, A U.S. PLANE TRANSPORTED THE BOLIVIAN PRESIDENT'S WIFE ON A EUROPEAN SHOPPING SPREE AT U.S. TAXPAYERS' EXPENSE.

BOLIVIAN OFFICERS WERE GIVEN TRAINING AT THE INFAMOUS SCHOOL OF THE AMERICAS.

THESE PAINFUL POINTS ON THE BODY ARE ESPECIALLY USEFUL IN HANDLING A CAPTIVE WHO MIGHT BE RELUCTANT TO GIVE INFORMATION.

EARLIER LAND REFORM MEASURES HAD ELIMINATED THE PEASANTS AS A POTENTIAL SOURCE OF SUPPORT.

IN DECEMBER 1966 TANIA BROUGHT GENERAL SECRETARY MÁRIO MONJE TO THE WELL-ORGANIZED CAMP TO DISCUSS SUPPORT OF THE GUERRILLAS BY THE BOLIVIAN COMMUNIST PARTY.

BUT THE MEETING WAS NOT SUCCESSFUL.

WE REFUSE TO JOIN ANY ARMED STRUGGLE NOT LED BY A BOLIVIAN.

BUT YOU DON'T UNDERSTAND. THIS IS JUST THE BEGINNING OF A GREAT GUERRILLA ARMY FROM ALL OF LATIN AMERICA!

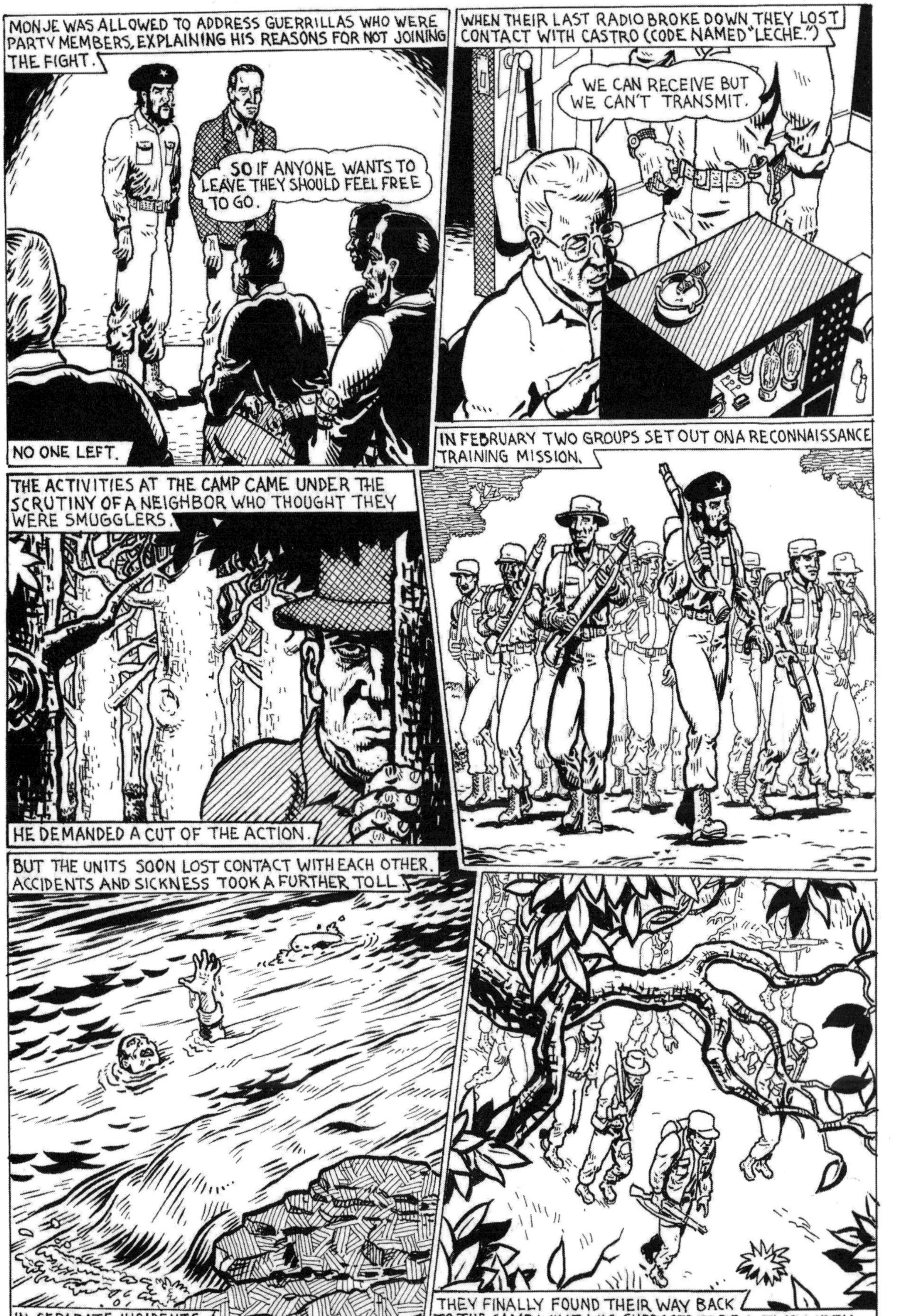

MONJE WAS ALLOWED TO ADDRESS GUERRILLAS WHO WERE PARTY MEMBERS, EXPLAINING HIS REASONS FOR NOT JOINING THE FIGHT.
SO IF ANYONE WANTS TO LEAVE THEY SHOULD FEEL FREE TO GO.
NO ONE LEFT.
WHEN THEIR LAST RADIO BROKE DOWN THEY LOST CONTACT WITH CASTRO (CODE NAMED "LECHE.")
WE CAN RECEIVE BUT WE CAN'T TRANSMIT.
THE ACTIVITIES AT THE CAMP CAME UNDER THE SCRUTINY OF A NEIGHBOR WHO THOUGHT THEY WERE SMUGGLERS.
HE DEMANDED A CUT OF THE ACTION.
IN FEBRUARY TWO GROUPS SET OUT ON A RECONNAISSANCE TRAINING MISSION.
BUT THE UNITS SOON LOST CONTACT WITH EACH OTHER. ACCIDENTS AND SICKNESS TOOK A FURTHER TOLL.
IN SEPARATE INCIDENTS TWO MEN DROWNED WHILE TRYING TO CROSS RIVERS.
THEY FINALLY FOUND THEIR WAY BACK TO THE CAMP. WHAT WAS SUPPOSED TO BE A TWO-WEEK TREK HAD TURNED INTO AN ORDEAL THAT LASTED 48 DAYS.

WHEN CHE RETURNED TO THE CAMP HE FOUND THAT TANIA HAD CLOSED THE URBAN OPERATION AND BROUGHT A VISITOR WITH HER.

HE'S FROM FRANCE. HIS NAME IS REGIS DEBRAY AND HE WANTS TO JOIN US.

CHE MADE CONTACT WITH THE MAOIST LEADER, A BOLIVIAN ALSO NAMED GUEVARA. HE STILL HOPED HE COULD SOMEDAY HEAL THE SINO-SOVIET RIFT.

OH YES, WE WILL BRING YOU ALL THE RECRUITS YOU NEED.

BUT YOU AND YOUR MEN WILL REMAIN RECRUITS UNTIL YOU PROVE YOURSELVES.

BUT THE MEN SENT BY THE BOLIVIAN MAOISTS HAD LITTLE TASTE FOR GUERRILLA LIFE. TWO IMMEDIATELY LEFT.

THEY SENT US THE DREGS!

THIS ISN'T THE WAY THEY TOLD US IT WAS GOING TO BE!

FOOEY!

ON THEIR WAY BACK THEY WERE CAPTURED BY THE ARMY AND REVEALED EVERYTHING THEY KNEW.

...AND THEY WERE LED BY A GUY THEY CALLED RAMON. HE SOUNDED CUBAN TO ME. THAT'S ALL I KNOW.

AN ARMY OBSERVATION PLANE BEGAN TO APPEAR IN THE SKIES AROUND THE CAMP.

THIS IS THE THIRD DAY THEY'VE BEEN FLYING AROUND UP THERE.

BLAM BZK KRANG POW

THEY BEGAN TO ENCOUNTER MORE ARMY PATROLS EVEN THOUGH THEY USUALLY FLED AT THE SIGHT OF CHE'S MEN.

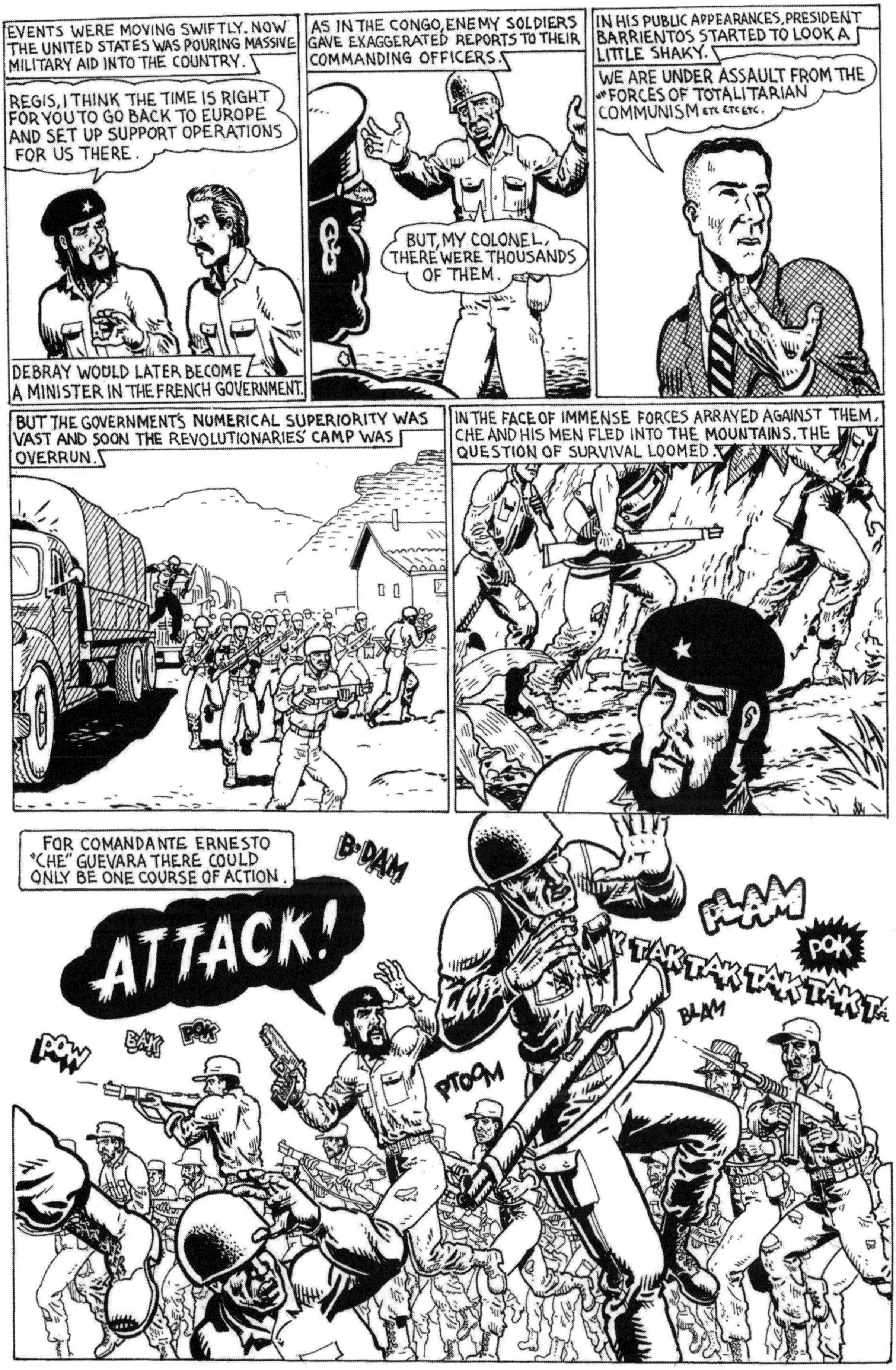
EVENTS WERE MOVING SWIFTLY. NOW THE UNITED STATES WAS POURING MASSIVE MILITARY AID INTO THE COUNTRY.
REGIS, I THINK THE TIME IS RIGHT FOR YOU TO GO BACK TO EUROPE AND SET UP SUPPORT OPERATIONS FOR US THERE.
DEBRAY WOULD LATER BECOME A MINISTER IN THE FRENCH GOVERNMENT.
AS IN THE CONGO, ENEMY SOLDIERS GAVE EXAGGERATED REPORTS TO THEIR COMMANDING OFFICERS.
BUT, MY COLONEL, THERE WERE THOUSANDS OF THEM.
IN HIS PUBLIC APPEARANCES, PRESIDENT BARRIENTOS STARTED TO LOOK A LITTLE SHAKY.
WE ARE UNDER ASSAULT FROM THE FORCES OF TOTALITARIAN COMMUNISM ETC ETC ETC.
BUT THE GOVERNMENT'S NUMERICAL SUPERIORITY WAS VAST AND SOON THE REVOLUTIONARIES' CAMP WAS OVERRUN.
IN THE FACE OF IMMENSE FORCES ARRAYED AGAINST THEM, CHE AND HIS MEN FLED INTO THE MOUNTAINS. THE QUESTION OF SURVIVAL LOOMED.
FOR COMANDANTE ERNESTO "CHE" GUEVARA THERE COULD ONLY BE ONE COURSE OF ACTION.
B-DAM
ATTACK!
PLAM
POK
TAK TAK TAK TAK TAK
BLAM
POW
BAM
POK
PTOOM

THE PRISONERS WERE RELEASED AND THE CAPTURED WEAPONS COUNTED. NOW IT WAS TIME TO MOVE ON.

AS THEY ASCENDED INTO THE MOUNTAINS THEY FOUND THE GOVERNMENT'S PROPAGANDA TEAM HAD DONE ITS JOB WELL.

THEY PRETEND TO PAY ME FOR THE FOOD BUT I KNOW THEY ARE BRUJAS* AND THE MONEY WILL DISAPPEAR SOON AFTER THEY LEAVE.

* BRUJAS = WITCHES

THEN CHE MADE A FATAL MISTAKE, BY DIVIDING HIS MEN INTO TWO GROUPS THEY BECAME MORE VULNERABLE.

BLAM
BAM
BLAM
BLAM

WOUNDED AND SICK, CHE WAS CAPTURED ON OCTOBER 8, 1967.

THE ASSASSIN STEPPED INTO THE DINGY SHED. CHE KNEW HIS LIFE WAS AT AN END. THE KILLER HESITATED.

SHOOT, COWARD. YOU ARE ONLY KILLING A MAN.

98

REGIS DEBRAY WAS CAPTURED BY BOLIVIAN POLICE BUT KEPT TO HIS STORY.

WHEN WILL YOU LET ME SLEEP? I TOLD YOU, I'M ONLY A REPORTER.

MUCH OF WHAT HAPPENED IN THOSE LAST DAYS WE KNOW THROUGH HIS ACCOUNTS.

A FEW OF CHE'S MEN EVADED CAPTURE AND MADE IT OUT.

A U.S. REPORTER INTERVIEWING FIDEL CASTRO ASKED HIM...

WHY DON'T YOU WANT TO HAVE GOOD RELATIONS WITH AMERICA?

NORMAL RELATIONS WOULD BE FINE WITH US. THAT QUESTION WOULD BE BETTER ADDRESSED TO YOUR OWN STATE DEPARTMENT.

LATER, THE REPORTER PUT THE SAME QUESTION TO A STATE DEPARTMENT OFFICIAL.

NORMALIZATION CAN ONLY OCCUR WHEN CUBA ALTERS ITS FOREIGN POLICY AND CHANGES ITS ECONOMIC SYSTEM.

IN OTHER WORDS, THE U.S. IS INCAPABLE OF SEEING CUBA AS A SOVEREIGN NATION.

BUT U.S. CONTEMPT WAS NOT CONFINED TO CUBA. IN THE NEXT DECADES THE U.S. WOULD HELP TO OVERTHROW ELECTED GOVERNMENTS WHILE PAYING LIP SERVICE TO DEMOCRACY.

BY NOW CHE'S MARTYRDOM HAD BECOME A POTENT RALLYING CALL FOR ALL THOSE WHO WOULD STAND UP TO IMPERIALISM, EVEN IN THE UNITED STATES.

NO

OUT NOW

OUT OF VIET NAM

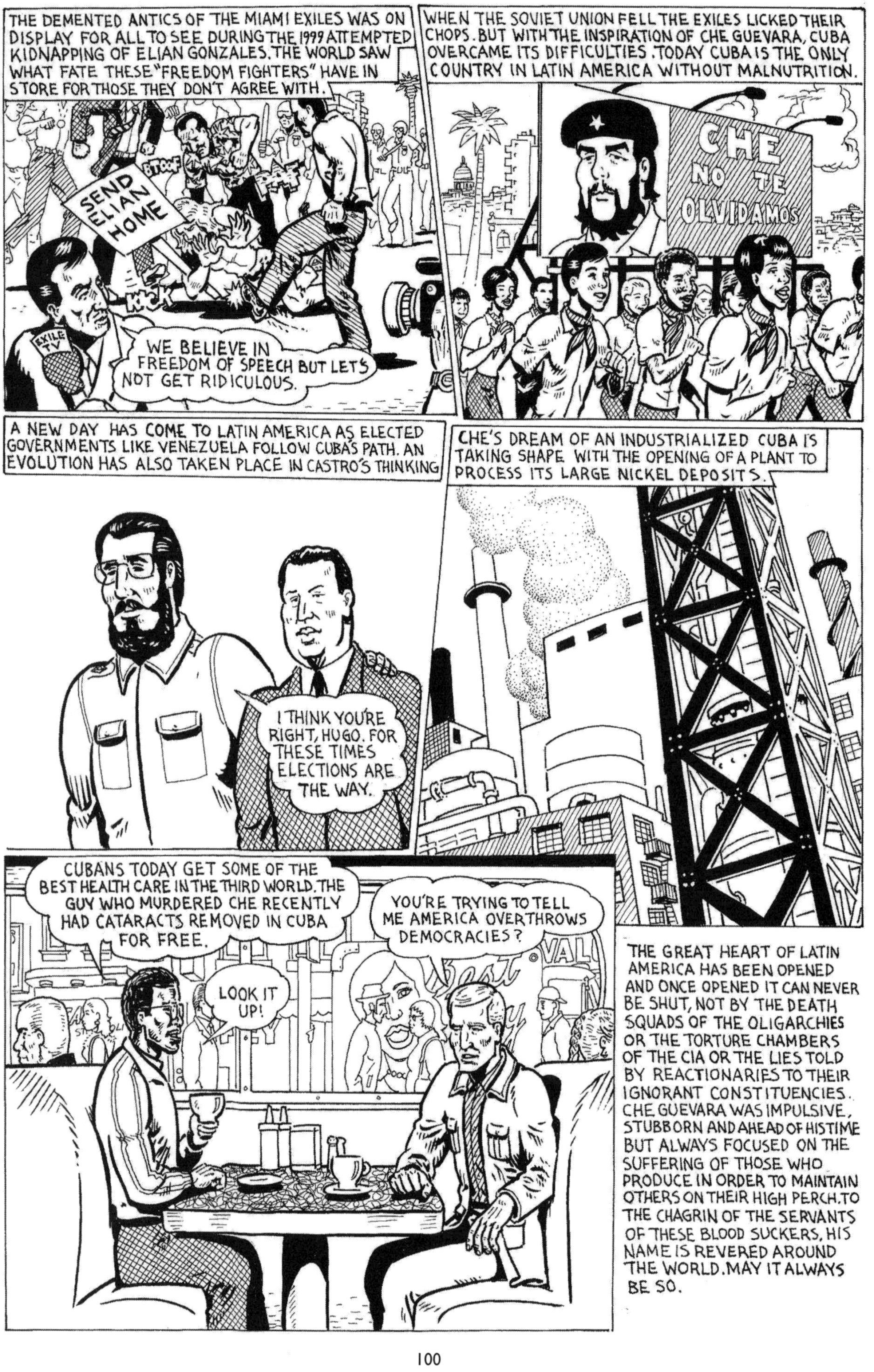

THE DEMENTED ANTICS OF THE MIAMI EXILES WAS ON DISPLAY FOR ALL TO SEE DURING THE 1999 ATTEMPTED KIDNAPPING OF ELIAN GONZALES. THE WORLD SAW WHAT FATE THESE "FREEDOM FIGHTERS" HAVE IN STORE FOR THOSE THEY DON'T AGREE WITH.
SEND ELIAN HOME
BTOOF
KICK
EXILE TV
WE BELIEVE IN FREEDOM OF SPEECH BUT LET'S NOT GET RIDICULOUS.
WHEN THE SOVIET UNION FELL THE EXILES LICKED THEIR CHOPS. BUT WITH THE INSPIRATION OF CHE GUEVARA, CUBA OVERCAME ITS DIFFICULTIES. TODAY CUBA IS THE ONLY COUNTRY IN LATIN AMERICA WITHOUT MALNUTRITION.
CHE NO TE OLVIDAMOS
A NEW DAY HAS COME TO LATIN AMERICA AS ELECTED GOVERNMENTS LIKE VENEZUELA FOLLOW CUBA'S PATH. AN EVOLUTION HAS ALSO TAKEN PLACE IN CASTRO'S THINKING
I THINK YOU'RE RIGHT, HUGO. FOR THESE TIMES ELECTIONS ARE THE WAY.
CHE'S DREAM OF AN INDUSTRIALIZED CUBA IS TAKING SHAPE WITH THE OPENING OF A PLANT TO PROCESS ITS LARGE NICKEL DEPOSITS.
CUBANS TODAY GET SOME OF THE BEST HEALTH CARE IN THE THIRD WORLD. THE GUY WHO MURDERED CHE RECENTLY HAD CATARACTS REMOVED IN CUBA FOR FREE.
YOU'RE TRYING TO TELL ME AMERICA OVERTHROWS DEMOCRACIES?
LOOK IT UP!
THE GREAT HEART OF LATIN AMERICA HAS BEEN OPENED AND ONCE OPENED IT CAN NEVER BE SHUT, NOT BY THE DEATH SQUADS OF THE OLIGARCHIES OR THE TORTURE CHAMBERS OF THE CIA OR THE LIES TOLD BY REACTIONARIES TO THEIR IGNORANT CONSTITUENCIES. CHE GUEVARA WAS IMPULSIVE, STUBBORN AND AHEAD OF HIS TIME BUT ALWAYS FOCUSED ON THE SUFFERING OF THOSE WHO PRODUCE IN ORDER TO MAINTAIN OTHERS ON THEIR HIGH PERCH. TO THE CHAGRIN OF THE SERVANTS OF THESE BLOOD SUCKERS, HIS NAME IS REVERED AROUND THE WORLD. MAY IT ALWAYS BE SO.

CHE GUEVARA, IMAGE AND REALITY

Sarah Seidman and Paul Buhle

Ernesto "Che" Guevara's image is everywhere. It adorns billboards in Cuba, towels in Italy, posters in Vietnam, record covers in the United States, cigarette packaging in Peru, and, most of all, t-shirts throughout in the world. Images of Che fill museums and inspire films, while contemporary celebrities have created personas and products to resemble the iconic Che. – Although Che Guevara died in 1967 at the age of 39, his image lives on. Every crisis of US empire, linked in particular to radical claims in Latin America, seems to expand his symbolic presence.

What does Che the image have to do with Che the person—anything, or everything? This book's format connects Che's life with his image. A look back on how Che's image has been used both as a concrete example of revolution and a vague symbol of rebellion—can shed light on who he was, and how his image has been used over time. While some authors have explored the visual power of Che iconography and others the historical significance of Che's life, few have combined these two elements, as Spain Rodriguez does here.

Images chronicle Che's life and shape his legacy. Photographs document his childhood in Argentina, his youthful travels through Latin America, his participation in the Cuban Revolution, his speech at the UN in 1964, and his fatal guerrilla activity in Bolivia. Drawings of Che from the Sierra Maestra in 1958 and on the cover of *Time* magazine in 1960 show the interest in Che and his image long before his cult status was established in the late 1960s. Photojournalist Freddy Alborta's widely circulated photograph of Che after his death in Bolivia helped cement his status as a martyr with a holy tinge.

Although many photographs of Che exist, one in particular helped spread his fame around the world. In 1960 Alberto Díaz Gutiérrez ("Korda"), a former fashion photographer working as a personal photographer for Fidel Castro, spontaneously snapped two frames of Che during the March 1960 mass funeral for the 80 victims of the La Coubre freighter explosion in Havana. Che assumed the United States was responsible for the explosion, and Korda captured his angry stare along with his beret, leather jacket and long hair. The photograph languished in relative obscurity until left-wing Italian publisher Giangiacomo Feltrinelli obtained a copy while visiting Korda's studio. Feltrinelli printed it onto posters disseminated throughout Europe just before Che's death in 1967, and the image multiplied exponentially in various formats and styles over the following years. This photograph has come to symbolize Che. It may possibly be, as widely claimed, the single most reproduced photograph of all time. Certainly, it is among the most recognizable of the twentieth century.

Images of Che come in many varieties. However, Che's typical uniform, first worn during the Cuban revolution, of military fatigues, beret with star, cigar and straggly beard, make him instantly identifiable. The endless images created out of Korda's photograph essentialize his features. In addition, the general popularity of political posters in the late 1960s created an arena for the popularity and dissemination of Che's image. But how do the components that go to make up the Che icon relate to episodes in his life?

Che lived by his own ideals of the "new man," the modern human being freed from the oppressions of the class system, who was ready to love, live and if necessary die for emancipation of humanity. He was a devout Marxist, a fervent proponent of international unity among oppressed peoples, and a believer in guerrilla warfare as a means of taking power; his ideas and prolific writings on these subjects reached people around the world. His socialist beliefs, struggles as a rural guerrilla, anti-imperialist stance and spirit of self-sacrifice, all of which combined the realms of action and intellect, captured the imagination of millions. The ideas that Che both advocated and embodied made him friends and enemies, and had a lasting impact on how people remember him and use his image. Jean-Paul Sartre called Che "the most complete human being of his age."

The Cuban revolution was a phenomenon that created iconic images and captured worldwide attention, and it was Che's participation in it that made him famous. Che's roles – first as a member of the expedition that sailed from Mexico for Eastern Cuba in the boat *Granma*; then as a military leader with the rank of comandante; and finally as a government leader in the justice tribunals, head of the Cuban Bank, and minister of industries – defined his status in the revolution: he was subordinate only to Fidel Castro. After his death, Castro notably used Che's image and example, rather than his own, to personify the Cuban revolution. To this day his features stare out from murals, memorials, buildings and billboards across Cuba.

The link between Che's fervent support of international unity, and the resulting globalization of his image, cannot be overstated. In addition to his youthful travels through Latin America, participation in the Cuban revolution and leadership of guerrilla campaigns in the Congo and Bolivia, Che traveled extensively during his tenure with the Cuban government through Africa, Asia, the Middle East and the Soviet bloc. His African military mission, a failure in itself, nevertheless set a path for a later and decisive Cuban victory in 1987–88 over CIA-supported mercenaries and South African troops that ended the invasion of Angola. That success set the timetable for the independence of Namibia from South Africa, and arguably changed the history of that continent. Through his writings, speeches and actions, Che advocated an alliance with oppressed peoples in Latin America, Africa and Asia, calling on them to unite in the fight against imperialism and "create two, three . . . many Vietnams."[1] He specifically advocated a united Latin America, calling the continent "a more or less homogenous whole," and using his

position in the Cuban government to train and fund left-wing guerrilla groups in countries including Argentina, Nicaragua and Peru.

Just as Che was an internationalist, his visual persona is an international phenomenon. Through Feltrinelli Korda's photograph was circulated in Italy; by 1968 student protesters brandished it; it adorned posters in Vietnam. Che was so recognizable that he had to travel from Cuba in disguise and adopt various identities. Ahmed Ben Bella, independence leader and former President of Algeria, recollected how a photograph of Che had sustained him during his time in prison, while poor rural women in Bolivia saved locks of his hair after his death as they might have preserved the relics of a holy martyr. Many Latin American Che posters juxtapose Che's image with the entire South American continent, such as Elena Serrano's "Day of the Heroic Guerrilla (Continental Che," and Patricia Israel and Alberto Pérez's "America Awakens," which was publicly burned during the Pinochet coup in Chile in 1973. Latin Americans in particular regarded him as a pan-Latin hero, martyr, and secular saint.[2]

While Che's exploits made him famous during his extraordinary lifetime, his death solidified his iconic status. His capture and execution at the age of 39 while fighting as a political insurgent in Bolivia instantly made him a martyr. The circumstances surrounding his death – CIA collaboration with the Bolivian government, the amputation of his hands before burial, and the exhumation of his "disappeared" body thirty years later, heightened the mysterious and martyred spectacle of Che. His untimely and violent death cast Che as a figure of mythic proportions.

To the late 1960s movements against the Vietnam War and for racial justice, gender equality and gay liberation in the United States, Che was an important posthumous icon for left-wing political, arts, and counterculture groups. Che posters adorned college dorm rooms, were carried at protests, and filled magazines and newspapers. Artist Rupert Garcia's 1968 print of Che with the words "Right On!," epitomizing the fusion of culture and politics of the time, was used in student strikes at San Francisco State College. During the late 1960s and early 1970s, the black power movement used his image to inspire armed struggle and

1 Ernesto Che Guevara, "Create Two, Three, Many Vietnams (Message to the Tricontinental)," April 1967, in Che Guevara *Reader: Writings on Guerrilla Strategy, Politics & Revolution*, ed. David Deutschmann (Melbourne: Ocean Press, 2003), 313.
2 David Kunzle, "Chesucristo: The Christification of Che," in *Che Guevara: Icon, Myth, and Message* (Hong Kong: South Sea International Press, 1997).

internationalism, while "Latino Brown Power" groups adopted him as a patron saint, and the student-led New Left regarded him as a symbol of the "new man."

Che's internationalism, socialism and theories of armed struggle made him an inspiring figure for the black power movement, in particular The Black Panther Party, founded in Oakland, California in 1966 by Huey P. Newton and Bobby Seale. The Black Panther Party monitored the police, ran political education classes and community survival programs, providing services such as free breakfast for schoolchildren. As well as drawing inspiration from the likes of Malcolm X, the Panthers placed strong emphasis on international socialist figures. The works of Che were required reading in the Panthers' political education classes, cited in speeches and writings, and his image was used as a symbol of unity among oppressed peoples worldwide, a unity badly needed by the hard-pressed Panthers.

Che's image, as well as his writing, was used to invoke the spirit of internationalism central to the Black Panther Party's ideology. Articles adorned with his picture often appeared in the *Black Panther* newspaper at this time, as did features about life in Cuba or Che's analysis of Vietnam. In August 1969, the *Black Panther* started a regular international news section, featuring a headline in bold lettering over a faint image of a machine gun and the images of Che Guevara, Ho Chi Minh, and Patrice Lumumba, and later Kim Il Sung and Mao Zedong. An October 1971 issue of the *Black Panther* marked the anniversary of Che's death with a special section devoted to the "The Week of the Heroic Guerrilla," as Che was known in Cuba.[3]

The Panthers' interest in Che also focused on his theories of guerrilla warfare. The group aroused controversy by proclaiming the rights of African-Americans to defend themselves against violence. On Che and Mao, Huey Newton wrote, "We read these men's works because we saw them as kinsmen; the oppressor who had controlled them was controlling us ... We believed it was necessary to know how they gained their freedom in order to go about getting ours."[4] The use of Che imagery and rhetoric by the Black Panthers, as well as the fact that Huey Newton and Eldridge Cleaver both lived in Cuba as political refugees, suggests that they looked to him not only as a symbol, but as a concrete example of an approach to create political change in the United States.

A range of Latino groups also identified with Latin American unity, the Cuban revolution and Che. Because many such groups sought alleviation of poverty, end discrimination, and to achieve independence from U.S. colonialism and imperialism, they embraced the Cuban revolution as a model and Che as an anti-colonial icon. Che was the subject of several themed murals, a form of Latino activism with a rich tradition in the United States and Latin America. These ranged from a 1971 mural of Che at the headquarters of the Young Lords Organization in Chicago to a 1978 mural of Che wearing a brown beret, entitled "We are Not a Minority!!," in the Estrada Courts housing project in Los Angeles. Images of Che abounded in Latino newspapers such as *Palante*, and at protest rallies.

The Young Lords in particular propagated Che's brand of anti-imperialism and appropriated his aesthetic style. In 1970 several Puerto Rican students in New York formed the Young Lords Party after declaring their autonomy from the Young Lords Organization, a Chicago street gang-turned political organization. The Young Lords Party closely identified with Che as a pan-Latin figure, and its original platform includes points such as "We are internationalists ... que vive Che Guevara!"[5] Members also fashioned themselves after Cuban revolutionaries, wearing military fatigues and Che's signature beret.[6] In this way, like other Latino groups such as the Chicano Brown Berets, the Young Lords Party members literally embodied Che's ideals.

Groups on the New Left also took interest in Che, using his image to express solidarity with the Cuban revolution, explore his theories of the "new man," and subvert conformity and question authority through youthful rebellion. While New Left support for Castro was at first uneven, ranging from adulation to resistance against romanticizing any Communist regime, through the 1960s the New Left came to embrace socialism as a political system and espoused a type of "Third World" Marxism that usually included ardent support for the Cuban Revolution and homage to the memory of Che. As the US military devastation of Vietnam increased and the

3 "The Week of the Heroic Guerrilla," *Black Panther* 7, no. 7, October 9 1971, 13.
4 Huey Newton, *Revolutionary Suicide* (New York: Harcourt Brace Jovanovich, 1973), 111.
5 Young Lords Party and Michael Abramson, *Palante: Young Lords Party* (New York: McGraw-Hill, 1971), 150.
6 Carmen Teresa Whalen, "Bridging Homeland and Barrio Politics: The Young Lords in Philadelphia," in *The Puerto Rican Movement: Voices from the Diaspora*, eds. Andrés Torres and José Velázquez (Philadelphia: Temple University Press, 1998), 112.

ideals of non-violence wavered, the New Left splintered into groups, some of whom advocated violence to achieve their aims. Solidarity with the Cuban Revolution and Che's persona grew both stronger and more contested.

One of the chief expressions of the New Left, the pan-US Students for a Democratic Society or SDS, in particular increasingly looked to Che. SDS's Port Huron Statement of 1962 offered a vision of "participatory democracy," an idea emphatically influenced by sociologist C. Wright Mills, a great admirer of and widely read commentator on the Cuban revolution. The appearance and rapid spread of the Underground Press – hundreds of local tabloids sold at low prices by street hawkers – demanded a proliferation of images, none more reproduced or idealized than Che. Significantly, neither Mao Zedong, to whom a section of SDS would become politically dedicated after 1969, nor Ho Chi Minh, whose name was evoked in one of the popular protest chants of the time ("Ho-Ho-Ho-Chi-Minh/Vietnam is going to win"), had his iconic pulling power. Che's image was diametrically opposed to those of Lyndon Johnson and Richard Nixon, whose faces were hatefully caricatured in cartoons, comic strips and posters. The New York-based arts magazine I-KON, which pioneered the use of Cuban-style art in the US, frequently depicted Che, and was soon slavishly copied by other magazines. Meanwhile, after an SDS delegation visited Havana in September 1968 to celebrate the 10th anniversary of the Cuban revolution, nearly every subsequent issue of the SDS newspaper New Left Notes featured reproductions of Cuban posters, animated cartoons and photographs of Che. SDS member Todd Gitlin wrote how "the courageous, noble, quixotic ghost of Che [was] looking over our shoulders in the dramas of the late sixties, as language shifted from 'protest' to 'resistance' and then to 'revolution.'"[7]

SDS and other New Left groups focused on Che both to explore and appropriate for their own purpose his idea of the "new man." I-KON remarked how Che embodies both the man of action and the intellectual, not only the fearless fighter but the romantic, even artistic, figure and lover.[8] That the New Left saw Che as a model human was evident in the Che posters featuring his quotation "At the risk of seeming ridiculous,

let me say that a true revolutionary is guided by feelings of love;" art historian David Kunzle writes that this poster was particularly popular in the United States with groups where armed struggle was a fantasy, but lovers numerous.[9] While the Weather Underground later looked to his image to justify their violent actions, SDS's use of Che had remained more romantic than anything else, focused upon love as much as struggle.

Che's rebellious nature and physical appearance became an aesthetic symbol for the 1960s counterculture. In 1969, an ad in the counterculture newspaper Berkeley Barb showed a man wearing an undershirt emblazoned with Che's image, suggesting a vision of rebellion as a mix of countercultural revolutionary expectation and consumer decision-making.[10] The following year, the back page of the Berkeley Tribe featured, among the yoga class, music and theater listings, a large mandala depicting brains, marijuana leaves, clenched fists, topless women – and Che.[11] This psychedelic combination of his image with drug paraphernalia and sexual liberation reinforced its presence in the pantheon of countercultural symbols. Controversy over Che and his image had increased when the publicity campaign for the 1968 cover of the left-leaning avant-garde literary magazine Evergreen Review, which featured a painting of Che by artist Paul Davis and the caption "The Spirit of Che lives in the new Evergreen!", resulted in the defacement of the posters in subway stations and the bombing of the Evergreen Review's offices in New York by persons unknown—as well as increased sales. Hoping to capitalize on the counterculture's interest in Che, Twentieth Century Fox released the major motion picture Che! in 1969, starring Omar Sharif as Che and Jack Palance as Fidel Castro. The original filmscript by the blacklisted screenwriter (and past Oscar winner) Michael Wilson, intended as a lionization of the great figure, had been ripped to shreds, the plot reconstructed with an evil, insane Che at its core. Appropriately, the film elicited terrible reviews and died at the box office.

Most New Left political groups that hadn't disbanded after 1970 following the devastating splits in the Students for a Democratic Society, the "underground" adventures of the Weathermen and the police and FBI suppression

7 Todd Gitlin, The Sixties: Years of Hope, Days of Rage (New York: Bantam Books, 1987), 282.
8 See I-KON 6 (October/November 1968), 3. The writer is presumably I-Kon editor, Susan Sherman.
9 Kunzle, Che Guevara: Icon, Myth, and Message, 85.
10 "Make Your Mother Happy. Buy an Undershirt," Berkeley Barb 9, no. 1, July 4–10 1969, 14.
11 Berkeley Tribe 2, no. 13, April 3–10 1970.

of the Black Panthers seemed to become disillusioned with Che's image, treating it as almost void of meaning. Activist Abbie Hoffman wrote that "Smoking dope and hanging up Che's picture is no more a commitment than drinking milk and collecting postage stamps," while SDS member Tom Hayden accused others of empty rhetoric by "leaving Che and Malcolm and Huey only as posters on their walls."[12] Rather than a clear shift from a universal, meaningful depiction of Che in the 1960s to a brazen commercial appropriation of him today, his image has continued to be utilized in many ways, and given many meanings.

After a lull in the late 1970s and 1980s amid the apparent exhaustion of the revolutionary political mood, Che's image is as ubiquitous today as in the years after his death. The combination of a 1990s fascination with all things '60s and the rise of the political-message t-shirt led to a resurgence in Che imagery. While his image still adorns dorm rooms and community murals, its presence on assorted consumer goods suggests its increased commercialization, decontextualization, and incorporation into celebrity culture. Many who see the image or wear the t-shirt don't know who Che was or what he did. Yet some still consider him a hero and powerful icon, and the continued controversy surrounding Che's life as revolutionary suggests that his image has not lost all meaning. The second-most popular image of radical or youthful rebellion, that of Bob Marley, remains alongside that of Che, a phenomenon that speaks for itself—and which may suggest that the mission of Latin America and the Caribbean, in global history, has yet to be fulfilled. Marley is the musical guerrilla to Che's military guerrilla, just as much opposed to neocolonialism and capitalism.

Che's increasingly commercialized image can now be found on key-chains, bikinis, cigarette packs, and even on the labels and advertisements for alcoholic drinks. Cuban contemporary art critic Gerardo Mosquera has decried the "complete commercial banalization" of Che, while before his death in 2001 Korda himself successfully sued Smirnoff vodka for using his image in an advertisement, saying: "As a supporter of the ideals for which Che Guevara died, I am not averse to its reproduction by those who wish to propagate his memory and the cause of social justice throughout the world, but I am categorically against the exploitation of Che's image for the promotion of products such as alcohol, or for any purpose that denigrates the reputation of Che."[13]

Attempts to associate his image with these products indicates that Che is perceived as attractive to youth: different, cool. Yet while he may now be associated with vague notions of rebellion rather than concrete theories of socialism or warfare, his placement on products says as much about a consumer culture, where nothing is off-limits or sacrosanct, as it does about Che's meaning.

Che's image has specifically been subjected to the postmodern pastiche that now characterizes mass culture. It is juxtaposed with images of other political figures or celebrities in new, self-conscious ways. Princess Diana, Cher, Ronald Reagan and Madonna all project iconic personalities that mimic Che. Artists create product-laden images of Che wearing iPod headphones or a Nike swoosh on his beret, while Che gear abounds on the internet. A t-shirt from Budapest depicts Che with the face of Mao Zedong as a deejay spinning a record, while a New Yorker cartoon portrays him wearing a Bart Simpson t-shirt. These products commodify Che, who is absorbed into the apathetic consumerist life to which he stood in revolutionary, romantic opposition. Yet they also deliberately play on the irony of his presence on consumer products, something that hints at a tacit recognition of the divergence between his own values and how his image is used.

Despite all this, Che is still viewed and represented as an idealized figure around the world. Venezuelan President Hugo Chávez, Bolivian President Evo Morales and other left-wing political leaders in Latin America extol Che's outspoken stance against US imperialism, and promote his image as a symbol of their Bolivarian revolution. In the United States and England, two separate exhibitions on Che imagery in the last decade have shown the continued prevalence and relevance of his image. David Kunzle argues that the rich artistic variety of Che images ensure their continued significance, while curator Trisha Ziff maintains that the image's sheer staying power suggests that it has significance even for those who know little about Che himself.[14] In 2007, countries around the world commemorated the fortieth anniversary of Che's death. Ceremonies attended by

12 Abbie Hoffman, *Steal This Book* (New York: Pirate Editions, 1971), v; Gitlin, *The Sixties*, 398.
13 Elizabeth Armstrong, "Che Chic; His Face Adorns the Banners of Guerrillas – and the Apparel of Hollywood Stars. Has the Iconic Image Usurped a Thrilling – and Tragic – Story?" in the *Christian Science Monitor*, March 5 2004, 13.
14 David Kunzle, Che Guevara and Trisha Ziff, *Che Guevara: Revolutionary & Icon* (New York: Abrams Image, 2006).

Latin American heads of state, pilgrimages to the site of Che's death, and eulogizing editorials in Zimbabwe to China all attest to the continuing impact of Che's global legacy.

Controversy surrounding both Che and his image continues, with no end in sight. Former New Left-turned-liberal critic Paul Berman attacked the depiction of the young Che in Walter Salles's 2004 film *Motorcycle Diaries*, arguing that it contributed to a larger trend that obscured Che's brutality and recklessness.[15] In October 2006 the *San Antonio Express-News* ran a news story about a city employee who was criticized for wearing a t-shirt with a picture of Che while riding her bike to work, even when the t-shirt turned out to be part of a fundraiser for a local radio station. The radio station's program director insisted, "We weren't taking a side on whether Guevara was a villain or a hero. We were just playing up the angle of 'revolutionary radio' . . . We weren't trying to make a political statement."[16] Amidst the continuing controversy around Che's life, use of his image has increasingly been defended as meaningless and harmless in order to justify its continued commercial exploitation.

Attempts to assign meaning to Che iconography today are eased by understanding its varied use in the past. Just as groups in the New Left, Latino communities and Black Power movement used Che's image in diverse ways during the 1960s and '70s, his image today is likewise considered both powerfully resonant and empty of meaning. That familiar photograph of Che now says as much about revolutionary movements in the past as it does about our current pervasive celebrity culture. As Spain Rodriguez's powerful artwork demonstrates, understanding Che's life and the development of his image are the first steps towards reclaiming its power to harness these transformative social forces at work around the globe today.

15 Paul Berman, "The Cult of Che: Don't Applaud the Motorcycle Diaries," *Slate*, September 24 2004.
16 Roddy Stinson, "'Chic Che' T-shirt Worn by City Employee Riles Neighbors Reader," *San Antonio Express-News*, October 26 2006, 3A.